PITTSBURGH
Chefs Cook Book

by Rosemary Walters

22 classic meals from the area's finest restaurants

Now you can enjoy Pittsburgh's best restaurants' cuisine in the comfort of your own home.

This is a cookbook for those who like to eat out but would love to take the great recipes they've experienced home with them. Whether you're a novice or accomplished chef, you'll enjoy creating a complete meal covering soups through desserts outlined in the pages of this cookbook that feature some of the finest restaurants in Pittsburgh.

Open the book and discover recipes to tantalize the palate from establishments such as Cafe Azure, Cheese Cellar, Klein's, The Prime House, Vernons and more! With this wide selection, you'll be able to please all types of tastes and will have a collection of recipes you'll use over and over.

CONTENTS

Arthur's Restaurant

Seafood Cocktail

Braciole

Heritage Pie

Arthur's Restaurant

Arthur's Restaurant is located in the historic Burke Building just off of P.P.G. Square in downtown Pittsburgh. Built in 1836, the building hosts two fireplaces in every dining room as well as an oak staircase of Edwardian design. The rich early-American decor is further enhanced by Arthur's famous Scotch bar that is a replica of the early bars in Colonial Williamsburg.

At Arthur's famous Scotch Bar, patrons are invited to experience the pleasures of over 275 scotches - hopefully, not all at one sitting. Periodically, Scotch tasting parties are hosted at Arthur's where invited guests yarn about the histories, ingredients and flavors of selected Scotches.

Add to this a menu of Beef Wellington, veal, seafood and Northern Italian cuisine and you have an ideal setting for a restaurant based on early-American tradition. Chuck Liberatore, owner and chef at Arthur's, invites you to come and savor the flavor of Arthur's, voted one of the top five in Pittsburgh by the Ambassador Club of Chicago for two years in a row.

209 4th Avenue
412/566-1735

Seafood Cocktail

1/4 pound scallops
1/4 pound shrimp
3/4 pound swordfish
1 red bell pepper, diced
End pieces of stock of
  scallions, chopped

2 pounds marinated artichoke
  hearts with juice
1/4 cup virgin olive oil
Dash of thyme
Salt and pepper
Dash of hot sauce
1/8 cup lemon juice

1. Boil off shrimp, scallops, and swordfish and let cool.

2. Mix other ingredients together with seafood and serve chilled. Makes 6 servings.

Braciole
(Serves One)

1 8-ounce sirloin strip
1 egg
Butter
Flour
1 clove crushed garlic

Fresh spinach, stemmed and
 washed
Prosciutto ham
Provolone cheese
2 tablespoons olive oil
Salt and pepper

1. Whisk an egg and panfry in a little butter until it sets.

2. "Butterfly" an eight ounce sirloin strip by slicing it horizontally almost all the way through (the meat should remain attached on one side).

3. Season the meat on both sides with salt and pepper, cover with wax paper and pound it thin.

4. Brush the beef with a clove of crushed garlic. Coat it with washed, stemmed spinach. On goes the egg, cooked to resemble an omelet. Crown it with thin slices of Prosciutto ham and Provolone cheese.

5. The whole thing is rolled up, tied with string and dusted with flour.

6. Saute in 2 tablespoons of olive oil until brown on all sides. Bake at 400 degrees for 5-7 minutes or longer depending on how long you want it cooked.

Heritage Pie

2/3 pound butter
1/8 cup Amaretto

1/8 cup Hershey's chocolate
 syrup
1/4 cup powdered sugar

1. Whip until light and fluffy, approximately 30 minutes.
2. Pour into graham cracker crust.
3. Set in freezer for several hours and serve.

The Back Porch

Dinner for Four
Charcoal Broiled Shrimp
Lemon Herb Vinaigrette Salad with Feta Cheese
Assorted Roll and Miniature Muffin Basket
Breast of Duck Chambord
Spaghetti Squash
Assorted Miniature Pastries

The Back Porch

The Back Porch Restaurant was opened in 1975, when Joseph and Sally Pappalardo, formerly of New Jersey, transformed the 1806 farmhouse into a charming and classy colonial dinner house. All three levels of one of the oldest buildings in Western Pennsylvania, built and owned by the prominent Speers family, is utilized by the Pappalardos for their stylish restaurant. The two dining rooms with fireplaces, the sunporch and the rathskeller are decorated with antiques and artifacts gathered from Southwestern Pennsylvania.

The Back Porch has become the place to take friends and celebrate special occasions. Lawn weddings, business meetings or intimate candlelight dinners by the fire are all enhanced by exquisite food prepared to order. The menu consists of European-American cuisine and features fresh seafood, milk-fed veal and Black Angus beef. All dessert and ice cream creations are made for the Back Porch and sold at the family owned Ice Cream Cafe "Jamies" located across the street.

Lunch is served daily Tuesday through Saturday and features salads, sandwiches and light fare entrees.

Interesting decor, excellent cuisine and attentive service make the Back Porch a food landmark.

114 Speers Street, Belle Vernon
412/483-4500

Charcoal Broiled Shrimp

16 large raw shrimp   *1 cup melted butter*

1. Peel and devein raw shrimp, leaving tails intact and refrigerate.

2. Brush cold shrimp with melted butter (butter will solidify onto cold shrimp).

3. Place buttered shrimp six inches above medium coals, moving frequently to avoid flare-up. Do not overcook, take off coals when shrimp are white throughout.

4. Serve warm with cold cocktail sauce.

Lemon Herb Vinaigrette Salad with Feta Cheese

1 large bunch leaf lettuce,   *Pinch of sugar*
  torn into bite size pieces   *2 egg yolks*
1 teaspoon chopped parsley   *3/4 cups olive oil*
1 teaspoon oregano   *1/4 cup vegetable oil*
1/2 teaspoon minced shallots   *1 cup sliced mushrooms*
1/2 teaspoon minced garlic   *1 cup crumbled Feta cheese*
Juice of one lemon   *Salt and fresh ground pepper*
4 tablespoons red wine vinegar   *to taste*

1. Combine parsley, oregano, shallots, garlic, lemon juice, vinegar and sugar in a bowl.

2. Whisk in slightly beaten egg yolks.

3. Slowly pour in olive oil and vegetable oil, whisking continually until thoroughly combined. Add salt and pepper.

4. Place lettuce on chilled plates and drizzle the dressing over. Garnish with mushrooms and Feta cheese.

Miniature Apple Muffins

1-3/4 cups flour
1-1/2 cups Mackintosh
apples, peeled and finely
chopped
1 cup sugar
1/2 teaspoon salt

1/2 teaspoon baking soda
1/2 teaspoon cinnamon
3/4 cup vegetable oil
1/2 cup chopped, toasted
walnuts
1/2 teaspoon vanilla

1. In large bowl, thoroughly combine flour, apples, sugar, salt, baking soda and cinnamon.

2. Stir in walnuts and vanilla.

3. Slowly stir oil into mixture.

4. Preheat oven to 350 degrees.

5. Place paper muffin cups into miniature muffin pans.

6. Fill each cup 2/3 full of muffin mixture.

7. Bake 15 minutes or until toothpick inserted in center comes out clean. Yield 2-1/2 to 3 dozen.

Breast of Duck Chambord

4 whole boneless duck breasts

1. Trim excess skin from the sides, removing about 50% of skin.

Marinade:
4 tablespoons chopped onion
4 tablespoons chopped celery
3 teaspoons sugar
2 teaspoons anise
1 teaspoon cinnamon
1/2 cup soy sauce
2 cups water

1. Add all ingredients in a stainless steel bowl.

2. Place trimmed duck breast in marinade overnight.

Chambord Glaze:
1/4 cup Chambord liqueur
1/4 cup pureed frozen
  raspberries
1/4 cup marinade
3/4 cup chicken stock
1 tablespoon cornstarch
1 tablespoon cold water
1/2 cup oil
1/2 cup butter

1. Heat Chambord, raspberries, marinade and chicken stock. Gradually stir in a paste made with 1 tablespoon cornstarch and 1 tablespoon water, increase heat, stirring until boiling. Take off heat and keep warm.

2. In a 12-inch skillet, add oil and butter, bring to a medium high heat. Cook duck breasts two at a time, skin side down, until skin is crisp, about 5 minutes. Turn and continue to cook an additional 5 minutes or until medium rare.

3. With electric knife in slanting position, carve in thin slices, keeping form of duck breast.

4. Place sliced breasts on warm plate and spoon over Chambord glaze.

Spaghetti Squash

1 4 x 8-inch spaghetti squash
1/4 cup butter

Salt and fresh ground pepper
to taste

1. Slice squash lengthwise and scoop out seeds.

2. Bake face down on buttered tray at 350 degrees for 30 minutes or until easily pierced with a fork. Cool until easy to handle.

3. Scrape out inside with a fork, creating spaghetti-like strands with a slightly crunchy texture.

4. Dot with butter and toss, add salt and pepper.

Opera Tarts

Cookie Dough:
2 sticks soft, unsalted butter
1/3 cup sugar

1 teaspoon vanilla
1 egg
2-1/2 cups flour

1. Beat butter and sugar until smooth. Add vanilla, then egg, blend in flour slowly.

2. With fingers, press dough into miniature muffin pans to form cups.

3. Bake in 350 degree oven 15 minutes - cool shells.

Tart Filling:
1 cup whipping cream
3 tablespoons sugar

1/2 teaspoon instant espresso
1 ounce semi-sweet chocolate

1. In heavy saucepan over low heat, bring whipping cream, sugar and espresso to a boil, stirring frequently to avoid scorching. Reduce to 3/4 cup.

2. Remove from heat, whisk in chocolate and let cool 10 minutes.

3. Fill pastry shells with warm filling and cool completely.

4. Place in paper cups and sprinkle with powdered sugar. Yield 2 dozen miniatures.

Cafe Azure

Dinner for Six
Oysters on the Half Shell with Sherry, Balsamic Vinegar,
and Cracked Black Pepper
Norwegian Salmon and Red Bell Pepper Cream Soup
Roasted Country Duck with a Maple Bourbon Sauce
Belgian Endive and Watercress with a Walnut Vinaigrette

Wine Suggestions:

Acacia Chardonnay "Marina Vineyard" 1986
Chateau Branaire - Ducru, 1978
Taylor Fladgate, Vintage Porto, 1978

Cafe Azure

Cafe Azure is considered Pittsburgh's premiere outdoor cafe and offers a diverse selection of Provincial and Nouvelle cuisine. For formal or intimate entertainment settings, one may choose the main floor dining room with piano bar or the private, elevated dining room of this elegantly renovated nineteenth century home.

The menu is imaginative and features dishes that are prepared in the French tradition and the American style. Since the overriding concern is quality, the menu changes seasonally in order to take maximum advantage of regional products. In fact, this philosophy of cuisine based on French tradition, American style, and freshest ingredients is the foundation of the SEASONS OF AZURE, Cafe Azure's year long tribute to seasonal dining.

The Cafe's contemporary decor and Erte silkscreens, which are on display throughout the restaurant, have created a subtle, relaxing atmosphere in which to enjoy a delightful culinary experience. Offering alfresco dining in season, Cafe Azure's professional staff is committed to excellence. To experience "a little bit of French cuisine", go to the corner of Craig and Filmore Streets in Oakland. Located only one block from The Carnegie, Cafe Azure celebrates seasonal dining throughout the year.

317 South Craig Street
412/681-3533

Robert Flory, Owner
Richard Willen, Chef

Oysters on the Half Shell with Balsamic Vinegar and Cracked Black Pepper

30 Blue Point oysters
30 teaspoons Balsamic vinegar

15 black peppercorns (crushed coarsely)
1/2 cup finely chopped parsley

1. Shuck oysters and discard top half of shell.

2. Pour 1 teaspoon Balsamic vinegar on each oyster.

3. Sprinkle with cracked black pepper.

4. Place in hot oven or broiler long enough to remove chill, about 30 seconds.

5. Sprinkle with fresh parsley and serve.

Norwegian Salmon and Red Bell Pepper Cream Soup

*1 pound fresh salmon filet (all
  bones removed), diced
2 medium red bell peppers
1 medium onion, diced
2 16-ounce cans clam juice*

*1 teaspoon tarragon
1 bay leaf
16 ounces heavy cream
4 tablespoons butter
5 tablespoons flour*

1. Place first six ingredients into a four-quart pot or saucepan. Bring to a boil and turn down to simmer for 30 minutes.

2. Remove from stove and strain. Reserve broth. Remove bay leaf and puree fish and vegetables in blender until smooth (may have to add half a cup of broth to puree).

3. Return stock, pureed fish and vegetables to pot and bring to a simmer.

4. Melt butter in small saucepan and stir in flour until smooth.

5. Using a wire whip, vigorously stir flour and butter mixture into simmering soup. Let simmer for 15 minutes (soup will thicken).

6. Add cream and simmer for 15 more minutes. Salt and white pepper to taste.

Cafe Azure

Roasted Country Duck with a Maple Bourbon Sauce

3 3-4 pound ducklings　　　　*Salt and white pepper*
(remove excess fat)

1. Place ducks on roasting rack with roasting pan. Season with salt and white pepper.

2. Place in 400 degree oven for 20 minutes; then reduce heat to 350 degrees. Cook for 40 more minutes or until ducks are browned.

3. Allow ducks to cool for 30 minutes. Cut in half and remove the spine and rib bones (they will pull out easily) and remove wing bones. Leave the drum part of the wing attached to the body.

To re-heat:

Place in 350 degree oven for 30 minutes and serve.

Maple Bourbon Sauce

1 cup Bourbon　　　　　　　*4 tablespoons butter*
1/2 cup pure Maple syrup　　*4 tablespoons flour*
1 tablespoon shallots, minced　*2 tablespoons duck pan*
16 ounce can beef broth　　　*drippings*
16 ounce can chicken broth

1. Place first three ingredients in a two quart saucepan and bring to a boil. Let reduce for 3-5 minutes.

2. Add beef and chicken broth and bring back to a boil. Turn down to a simmer.

3. Melt butter in small saucepan and stir in flour until smooth.

4. Using a wire whip, stir flour and butter mixture into sauce until dissolved, let simmer for 15-20 minutes. Sauce will thicken. Serve.

15

Cafe Azure

Belgian Endive and Watercress with a Walnut Vinaigrette

5 bunches watercress   *4 Belgian endive*

1. Chop watercress and endive coarsely and toss lightly with vinaigrette.

2. Divide among six plates and top each salad with remaining vinaigrette.

Vinaigrette Dressing:
1/2 cup walnuts
4 tablespoons red wine vinegar
1 teaspoon DiJon mustard

1/2 cup walnut oil
1/3 teaspoon fresh ground
  black pepper
1/2 teaspoon salt

1. Chop walnuts into coarse pieces.

2. Combine oil with vinegar and add remaining ingredients. Whip until well blended.

The Carlton

Dinner for Six
Saffron Fettuccine with Sauteed Sea Scallops
and Roasted Red Pepper Beurre Blanc
Frisee and Mache with Bacon, Golden Raisins
and Lemon Shallot Vinaigrette
Roasted Veal Chops with West Virginia Goat Cheese,
Sage and Sun Dried Apricot Sauce
Mocha Creme Brulee Tart

Wine:

With Fettuccine - 1981 Trefethen Library Selection
Chardonnay
With Veal Chops - 1985 Napa Valley Duckhorn Merlot

Stephen J. Saenz, Chef

The Carlton

The Carlton Restaurant, at One Mellon Bank Center in Pittsburgh, has been upholding the fine dining tradition since its opening in November of 1984. Founded by the Levy Restaurants of Chicago in partnership locally with Managing Partner, Kevin Joyce, The Carlton has been well received by the Pittsburgh dining public.

Chef Stephen Saenz has crafted an ever-changing menu that one critic says is "consistent, innovative and judiciously seasoned". Mike Kalina has called The Carlton "the best downtown has to offer", and The Carlton has been acclaimed in national publications such as Esquire, Food and Wine, and the Mobil Travel Guide.

The Carlton enjoys an excellent lunch and dinner business. Its evening customers have come to appreciate the complimentary parking in One Mellon Bank Center and the theater crowd enjoys the complimentary round-trip limousine service to Heinz Hall and Benedum Center. The Carlton offers an unforgettable dining experience in an elegant atmosphere.

One Mellon Bank Center
412/391-4099

Saffron Fettuccine with Sauteed Sea Scallops and Roasted Red Pepper Beurre Blanc

2-1/3 cups flour
1/2 teaspoon salt
2 eggs
1/3 cup water
1 teaspoon olive oil
1 teaspoon saffron powder
2-1/4 pounds sea scallops

3 large red bell peppers
(roasted in oven and skin removed)
1/4 cup vermouth
2 shallots, chopped
1-1/2 pints heavy cream
1-1/4 pound butter, soft

1. Mix flour and salt.

2. Make well in center and pour in eggs, oil, and saffron dissolved in water.

3. Knead dough for 10 minutes. Let rest for one hour and cut into fettuccine pasta.

4. Cook pasta until tender, keep warm.

5. Place shallots and vermouth in saucepan and reduce until 2 teaspoons remain, add cream and reduce by 1/3, whip in soft butter and pureed bell peppers.

6. Coat scallops with flour and saute in butter until done.

7. Toss with pasta and sauce. Garnish with fresh chopped red pepper.

Frisee and Mache with Bacon, Golden Raisins and Lemon Shallot Vinaigrette

3 bunches frisee
1/2 pound mache
1/2 pound bacon, chopped
  and cooked
1/2 cup golden raisins

2 shallots, chopped
Juice of two lemons
1/2 cup olive oil
Salt and pepper
Pinch sugar

1. Clean lettuce and toss with bacon and raisins.

2. Mix shallots, lemon juice, olive oil, salt, pepper and sugar.

3. Pour dressing over greens.

Roasted Veal Chops with West Virginia Goat Cheese,

Sage and Sun Dried Apricot
  Sauce
6 10-ounce veal chops, center
  cut
1 pound West Virginia goat
  cheese

1 bunch fresh sage, chopped
Salt and pepper
1/4 pound dried apricots,
  chopped
1 quart veal stock, demi glazed
1/4 pound butter

1. Preheat oven to 400 degrees.

2. Cut pockets in veal chops.

3. Mix goat cheese, sage with salt and pepper.

4. Stuff chops with cheese mixture.

5. Saute in butter until light brown on outside.

6. Roast in oven for 7 minutes.

7. Cook apricots with veal stock for 15 minutes at simmer, whip in butter. Serve over chops.

Mocha Creme Brulee Tart

1 quart whipping cream
1/4 cup sugar
1 tablespoon vanilla
2 tablespoons instant coffee
dissolved in 3 tablespoons
water

9 egg yolks
1 pastry tart shell in metal
liner
Dark brown sugar

1. Preheat over to 350 degrees.

2. Combine first four ingredients in heavy saucepan and warm slowly over low heat (180 degrees).

3. Beat eggs until lemon colored.

4. Slowly pour hot cream into yolks, mix gently.

5. Pour into tart shell and bake 25-30 minutes.

6. Refrigerate overnight.

7. Top with brown sugar and broil to melt sugar, be careful not to burn. Serve after cool.

Cheese Cellar

Cheese Fondue

Corn Chowder

Tossed Salad with Honey Mustard Peppercorn Dressing

Chicken Fettucini

Chocolate Fondue

Cheese Cellar

The casual, friendly atmosphere makes this a favorite gathering place for dining and cocktails. The diverse menu features fresh seafood and pasta specials that change daily as well as burgers, chicken, sandwiches, stir-frys, salads and more. The Cheese Cellar also offers an extensive wine list. We're open seven days for lunch, dinner, late night snacks and Sunday buffet brunch.

#25 Shops at Station Square
412/471-3355

Swiss Cheese Fondue
(Serves Four)

1 whole garlic clove
1-1/2 cups Chablis
1 tablespoon lemon juice
1/2 pound Emmenthal
cheese, grated

1/2 pound Gruyere cheese,
grated
2 teaspoons cornstarch
3 tablespoons Kirsch
Few grains cayenne
Few grains nutmeg

1. Rub inside of 1-quart fondue pot with cut surface of garlic.

2. Pour Chablis and lemon juice into fondue pot.

3. Heat wine and lemon juice until it begins to steam, but do not boil.

4. Combine Emmenthal, Gruyere and cornstarch. Toss to combine.

5. Add cheese to wine in small amounts, stirring constantly with a wooden spoon, until cheese is melted.

6. Add Kirsch, cayenne and nutmeg after last amount of cheese is added, stirring constantly.

7. Bring to a boil. Serve immediately with cubes of French bread, apple slices or fresh vegetables.

Corn Chowder

2-1/2 cups raw potatoes,
  peeled and diced
6 slices bacon, cut fine
3 tablespoons onions, chopped
  fine

2 cups crushed corn, canned
  or fresh
3-1/2 cups milk
1 teaspoon salt
Dash pepper
1/2 cup cream, 18%

1. Cook potatoes and onions in boiling water. Drain.

2. Saute bacon, drain off excess fat.

3. Combine potatoes, bacon, corn and milk. Add seasonings and cook slowly together for 8-10 minutes. Add cream just before serving.

Tossed Green Salad with
Honey Mustard Peppercorn Dressing

*2 cups tossed greens (head
lettuce, Romaine, Bibb,
Spinach, etc.)
2 tablespoons carrots, grated
2 slices cucumber, 1/4 inch
1 tomato wedge
1 ripe olive*

*2 tablespoons red cabbage,
shredded
2 Pita chips, deep-fried or
oven-crisp
3 tablespoons Honey Mustard
Peppercorn Dressing**

1. In a chilled glass salad bowl, place tossed greens.

2. On left side of bowl, place carrots, cucumber, tomato and olive. Place cabbage along side the vegetables, toward the center of the bowl.

3. Between the vegetables and the side of the bowl, place Pita chips.

4. Ladle dressing over the right side of the tossed greens.

*Honey Mustard Peppercorn Dressing

*1 pint Peppercorn Marzetti
dressing*

*3/8 cup honey
1/4 cup Gulden's mustard*

1. Combine all ingredients; blend well.

2. Chill for service.

NOTE: Prepare dressing one day in advance of service to blend flavors.

Spinach Fettucini with Chicken
(Serves Two)

2 tablespoons clarified butter
1 piece boneless chicken breast, cut into strips
2 tablespoons flour, seasoned with salt, pepper and tarragon
1 tablespoon green onion, diced

1/4 cup mushrooms, sliced
2 teaspoons lemon juice
1/2 cup heavy cream
2 cups spinach fettucini, cooked
1/4 cup Parmesan cheese
2 tablespoon tomatoes, diced

1. Heat butter in skillet.

2. Dredge chicken pieces in seasoned flour mixture. Shake off excess and saute for 20-30 seconds.

3. Add green onions, mushrooms and lemon juice. Continue to saute until chicken is lightly browned.

4. Add cream, pasta, Parmesan cheese and tomatoes. Stir gently to combine thoroughly. Simmer until cream is thickened.

5. Serve with toasted, chopped walnuts sprinkled over top.

Chocolate Fondue with Fruit and Cake

Chocolate Sauce:
1/2 cup butter
6 ounces unsweetened
 chocolate
1-1/2 cups sugar

1 cup Half-and-Half cream
1/8 teaspoon salt
1/4 cup plus 2 tablespoons
 orange flavored liqueur

1. In saucepan, melt butter and chocolate over low heat.

2. Add sugar, Half-and-Half and salt.

3. Bring to a boil, cook over medium heat at a slow rolling boil, stirring constantly for 5 minutes until thickened. Cover and refrigerate until needed.

4. When ready, heat chocolate sauce in microwave 20-30 seconds.

5. Add liqueur and stir to combine thoroughly. Serve immediately with fruit and cake.

For Service:

Pound cake, 1-1/4 inch cubes
Bananas, 3/4 to 1 inch chunks

Fresh fruit, 3 selections from
 list below
Marshmallows

For two:

1. Pour one cup warm Chocolate Sauce into dessert fondue pot and place over burner. On a dinner plate, attractively arrange pound cake cubes, bananas, fresh fruit, and marshmallows. Serve with two fondue forks and two dessert plates.

Fresh Fruits: (select 3 types that vary in color and shape)

Apples, unpeeled, 1-1/2 to 2
 inch chunks
Sweet cherries with stems
Tangerines, whole sections
Peaches, peeled, 1-1/2 to 2
 inch chunks

Pears, unpeeled, 1-1/2 to 2
 inch chunks
Pineapple, peeled, sticks or
 wedges
Strawberries, whole

Christopher's Restaurant

Trio of Roasted Peppers
Filetti Fisarmonica
Carpaccio Christopher's
Shrimp in Garlic Cream

Christopher's Restaurant

Christopher and Catherine Passodelis, the owners of Christopher's Restaurant, are proud of their staff and their accomplishments in the City of Pittsburgh and Western Pennsylvania. In our 17th year, we have received numerous awards for our cuisine and our fine wine selection.

Christopher's is high above the City of Pittsburgh, a rooftop restaurant that is serviced by an exterior glass elevator. The restaurant itself has the tallest glass walls in the country, being approximately 22 feet high from floor to ceiling. It is the only restaurant in the country that has three glass walls and one wall made completely of 20 tons of coal. The whole motif is of the City of Pittsburgh and Western Pennsylvania.

We are proud of our chef, Douglas Zimmerman and his accomplishments. We are also very proud of George Mahramas, our maitre d', who was formerly the lead singer of the Four Coins. He has been our maitre d' since we opened, approximately 17 years ago. He is well known throughout the area as well as the country because of being such a talent in the music world.

An evening at Christopher's is unusual in that we have a strolling violinist and pianist to play selections for our patrons. We have party rooms, two lounges and a beautiful view of a beautiful city.

1411 Grandview Avenue
412/381-4500

Trio of Roasted Peppers
(Appetizer)

6 red bell peppers (sweet)
6 cubanella peppers
  (semi-sweet)
1 yellow banana pepper (hot)
1-1/4 cups olive oil
4 anchovies, pasted
3 cloves garlic, minced
2 tablespoons capers
1/4 cup sliced black olives
1/4 cup red wine vinegar
Juice from 1 fresh lemon

2 tablespoons fresh oregano,
  chopped
2 tablespoons fresh basil,
  chopped
2 tablespoons fresh parsley,
  chopped
Salt and pepper
Crusty Italian bread
Butter
Parsley for garnish

1. Cut stem from peppers and remove seeds.

2. Rub peppers with a small amount of vegetable oil, just to coat.

3. Place peppers on a foil covered pan or sheet (this will make clean up MUCH easier).

4. Put peppers in an oven which has been preheated to its maximum temperature.

5. Roast peppers until well charred.

6. Remove peppers from oven, place into a paper bag and cool at room temperature.

7. Peel the peppers.

8. Saute pasted anchovies and garlic in a small amount of olive oil.

9. Add the capers and herbs and saute for a minute more.

10. Remove from heat.

11. Add and mix well the vinegar, remaining olive oil, lemon juice, and olive slices.

12. Season dressing to taste.

13. Place the peppers in a non-reactive container, cover with the marinade and let sit in refrigerator for at least 24 hours.

14. Artfully arrange three peppers (one of each type) on each plate.

15. Emulsify the remaining dressing/marinade by stirring it well.

16. Dress the peppers with a small amount of this emulsion, being careful to capture and utilize the garnish within the marinade.

17. Garnish the plate with a parsley sprig and small piece of buttered, crusty Italian bread. Yield 6 servings.

Developed 7/3/87 by Douglas Zimmerman, Executive Chef
Christopher's Restaurant, Pittsburgh, Pennsylvania

Filetti Fisarmonica

12 2-ounce medallions of
  tenderloin
2 medium tomatoes
12 ounces Mozzarella
  (preferably imported buffalo
  mozzarella)

1/2 pound basil or spinach
  pasta
Salt and pepper

1. Make Provencal Sauce (recipe below).

2. Grill or broil medallions to rare, turning once.

3. Season with salt and pepper, then place on broiler pan.

4. Skin and seed tomatoes (core stem ends, cut a small "x" on the opposite ends, submerge the tomatoes into boiling water for 30 seconds, then plunge the tomatoes into ice water - the skin should now easily peel from a ripe tomato). Cut the tomatoes in half horizontally and gently squeeze each half in order to just force out seeds without damaging the tomatoes.

5. Slice each tomato half into 3 nice slices.

6. Place a tomato slice over each medallion.

7. Cut the Mozzarella cheese into 12 pieces such that they are approximately 1/4 inch thick and fit nicely on top of each medallion and tomato slice.

8. Cook the pasta al dente, drain and divide between four warm plates.

9. Place constructed medallions under the broiler until cheese is melted and browning.

10. Ladle sauce over each plate of pasta and place three medallions in a row over the top of the sauce.

Christopher's Restaurant

Provencal Sauce

2 anchovies
1 strip bacon
1 clove garlic
1/4 cup olive oil
1 medium onion, diced

1 29-ounce can crushed
 tomatoes
1/2 teaspoon fennel seed
1/2 teaspoon salt

1. In blender, puree anchovies, bacon and garlic.

2. Pour blended mixture into a heavy pot, heat, add diced onion and saute until onions are translucent.

3. Add tomatoes, fennel seed and salt.

4. Simmer for 20 minutes, stirring occasionally.

Carpaccio Christopher's

1 pound New York strip sirloin

1. Make dressing (recipe below).

2. Completely trim meat of all fat and sinew leaving only the eye of the strip loin completely lean.

3. Place meat in the freezer for approximately 20 minutes until very firm, but not completely frozen.

4. Carefully slice the meat, in the same direction steaks would be cut, as paper thin as possible (if slices are not thin enough or are of uneven thinness, pound them gently between two sheets of wax paper using the smooth side of a meat mallet).

5. Divide and lay the meat slices in fans on four chilled plates.

6. Brush or evenly spread dressing over meat slices.

7. Lay marinated mushroom slices decoratively over carpaccio.

Dressing

4 large mushrooms, thinly sliced
1 lemon
1/2 teaspoon fresh garlic, minced
1/4 cup olive oil
2 teaspoons fresh basil, chiffonade cut

1 teaspoon fresh parsley, chopped
1/2 teaspoon DiJon mustard
Pinch salt
Pinch fresh cracked black pepper

1. Squeeze the juice of lemon into bowl.

2. Add all remaining ingredients, but mushroom slices, and whisk together well.

3. Very gently, saute mushroom slices and place into the dressing to marinade.

Christopher's Restaurant

Shrimp in Garlic Cream

*32 jumbo shrimp
(approximately 2 to 2-1/2
pounds)
1 tablespoon plus 1/4 cup
butter
1 tablespoon fresh garlic,
finely minced*

*1/2 teaspoon fresh lemon juice
1/4 cup dry white wine
3 cups heavy whipping cream
1/2 pound fettucini
1 cup leek greens, sliced
1/2 grated Parmesan cheese*

1. Peel, devein and clean the shrimp and split lengthwise.

2. Bring a large pot of salted water to a boil.

3. Utilizing 1 tablespoon of butter, saute the minced garlic gently in a large skillet, for about 1 minute (do not brown).

4. Add lemon juice, white wine, cream and shrimp to the skillet of garlic.

5. Bring to a gentle boil, applying such heat as to gently reduce the cream by evaporation without allowing the mixture to boil over (stirring occasionally helps prevent this).

6. Add pasta to boiling water and cook al dente, drain.

7. Divide pasta between four warm plates.

8. The cream and shrimp mixture should continue boiling until it reduces to a thick, luxurious sauce (should it reduce too far and "break", add 1 tablespoon water and shake pan).

9. A couple of minutes before you feel the sauce will have reduced to the thickness desired, add the leek greens, grated Parmesan cheese and remaining 1/4 cup butter.

10. Stir to incorporate well.

11. Divide shrimp and cream sauce over the dishes of pasta.

Cross Keys Inn

Dinner for Six

Veal Soup Kittanning

Salmon En Phyllo

Country Herbed Salad with Piccalilli Dressing

Breast of Duck Woodsman

Rum Raisin Cheesecake of the Inn
or
Almond Tart À La Cross Keys

Wines:

Eberle Chardonnay
Georges Duboeuf Beaujolais Villages

John L., Dorothy Jean, and Leonard T. Petrancosta
Proprietors

Michael Babines C.E.C. Chef

Cross Keys Inn

The Cross Keys Inn, now officially designated as an historic landmark, first welcomed guests more than a century ago.

In its early years, the Inn served as a "way station" between Pittsburgh and Kittanning - a haven beckoning weary travelers during an arduous 44-miles journey. Later, it became a central meeting place for area residents (as well as the scene of many a hoedown), then a familiar local taproom before it was beset by disrepair.

Today, after careful and authentic restoration, it once again extends a gracious welcome to guests. Inside, one can relax in the cheerful, home-like ambience of a traditional country inn while savoring untraditional foodstuffs.

Outside, the sign of the Cross Keys swings just as it must have in 1850.

In addition to lunch, dinner and Sunday brunch, the Cross Keys offers a unique atmosphere for client and business functions.

Experience Splendid Dining
in the 19th Century Manner

599 Dorseyville Road, Fox Chapel Section
412/963-8717

Veal Soup Kittanning

1/4 cup plus 1 tablespoon
  salad oil
1 pound veal leg, milkfed,
  medium diced
1 pint plus 1 cup water
1/2 teaspoon beef base
1/2 teaspoon chicken base
2 ounces clarified butter
1 cup celery, fine diced
1 cup whole onions, fine diced
1 cup carrots, fine diced

1 tablespoon fresh parsley,
  minced
1/4 teaspoon marjoram
1/4 teaspoon leaf thyme
1/8 teaspoon ground nutmeg
1 bay leaf
3 grams salt
3 grams white pepper
32 ounces espagnole sauce
2 eggs
1/4 cup whole pimento, fine
  diced

1. Saute veal cubes in a saucepan until evenly browned.

2. Combine the next three ingredients to make stock and add to the veal. Simmer and reduce until 1/2 cup of liquid remains.

3. Meanwhile, saute vegetables and spices until vegetables are al dente.

4. Combine sauteed vegetables with veal and add brown sauce. Simmer for 10 minutes and remove bay leaf.

5. Beat two eggs and strain into soup through a china cup stirring constantly.

6. Bring to a simmer and serve immediately. Serves 16.

Salmon En Phyllo

6 sheets Phyllo dough sheets,
thawed
4 ounces clarified butter
12 ounces salmon filets
6 ounces Spinach Herb
Filling*, 1 ounce portion (see
recipe)

6 leaves of leaf lettuce, cleaned
6 ounces Creme Fraiche*, 1
ounce portion (see recipe)
6 lemon wedges
6 fresh parsley sprigs, cleaned

1. Place a sheet of phyllo onto a smooth work surface. Lightly brush it with clarified butter. Place another sheet directly on top of the first and brush again. Place the third and final sheet on top of the first two and again, brush it lightly with the butter.

2. Evenly place six, 1 ounce pieces of salmon along the long edge of the buttered phyllo sheets.

3. Top each piece with 1/2 ounce of spinach herb filling*.

4. Cut the phyllo sheets into 6 even rectangles (short-way) and fold each rectangle as you would a flag being sure to completely seal in the salmon and filling. A triangle being the finished result.

5. Brush each triangle with butter.

6. Place 2 appetizer phyllos on a sizzle plate and bake at 425 degrees until golden brown.

7. Transfer the cooked phyllos to a service plate and garnish with leaf lettuce and creme fraiche*.

NOTE: The directions provide 3 servings, follow steps one through six again to serve six.

*Spinach Herb Filling

1/4 ounce chopped shallots
3/4 clove garlic, mashed
3/4 ounce margarine
6 ounces frozen chopped
* spinach, thawed and drained*
1/8 teaspoon leaf tarragon,
* crumbled*

1/16 cup parsley flakes,
* chopped*
1-1/2 teaspoon lemon juice
1/8 cup Anisette liqueur
1/4 teaspoon black pepper
1/4 teaspoon salt

1. In a skillet, melt margarine and saute shallots and garlic until soft.

2. Combine thawed spinach with the next 6 ingredients.

3. Add the sauteed vegetables to the spinach mixture and mix well. Chill and reserve for service.

*Creme Fraiche

1/2 cup sour cream

1/2 cup heavy whipping
* cream*

1. Mix together both ingredients until smooth.

2. Store in a one gallon glass jar.

3. Allow this mixture to stand in a warm area of the kitchen for 18 hours.

4. Chill and reserve for service.

Country Herbed Salad with Piccalilli Dressing

1-1/3 heads hydroponic bibb
lettuce, torn
1/3 head romaine lettuce, torn
2/3 head Belgian endive
lettuce, broken
1-1/2 head curly endive
lettuce, broken
2/3 head radicchio lettuce,
torn
1/6 cup fresh dill weed,
chopped

1/2 cup fresh basil, chopped
1/3 cup fresh tarragon,
chopped
1/3 cup fresh chives, chopped
1/3 cup fresh parsley, chopped
1/3 quart fresh celery leaves,
chopped
1/3 quart watercress, chopped
1/3 pound fresh spinach, torn

1. Clean and gently toss all ingredients. Serve with Piccalilli Dressing*.

*Piccalilli Dressing

2 eggs
1 quart salad oil
11 ounces green tomato
Piccalilli relish

1/4 cup white vinegar
6 ounces Grey Poupon Dijon
mustard dressing

1. Place eggs in mixer on medium-high speed until creamy yellow and thickened.

2. Gradually add oil in a steady stream to emulsify.

3. Add remaining ingredients and mix well.

4. Chill and hold for service.

Breast Of Duck Woodsman

9 ounces clarified butter
6 breasts BL/SL duck,
   cleaned
12 tablespoons all-purpose
   flour

1-1/2 cup brandy
36 ounces Woodsman Sauce*
60 ounces angel hair pasta
6 teaspoons fresh parsley,
   minced

1. Heat butter to a sizzle in a skillet.

2. Jacard, then dredge the duck breasts in flour and add to skillet.

3. Brown on one side then turn. Deglaze with brandy.

4. Add Woodsman Sauce* and toss until breast is coated. Finish in the oven.

5. Heat pasta in microwave and spread out onto serving plate. Top pasta with duck and sauce. Garnish with parsley.

*Woodsman Sauce

2 ounces clarified butter
1/4 cup chopped shallots
8 ounces wild mushrooms,
   sliced
2 tablespoons brandy
1/4 cup sherry

3/8 teaspoon ground cloves
1/8 teaspoon salt
1 teaspoon white pepper
8 ounces cream sauce
1 pint heavy whipping cream

1. Heat butter in a heavy saucepan, saute shallots al dente and lightly browned.

2. Add mushrooms and again cook until al dente.

3. Deglaze the pan with the brandy and sherry, then reduce by 1/2.

4. Add the remaining ingredients and simmer for 5 minutes.

5. Reserve for service.

Cross Keys Inn

Rum Raisin Cheesecake

1-1/2 cups graham cracker
 crumbs
1/2 cup granulated sugar
1/2 cup margarine, melted
1 pint water
1 cup raisins
2 pounds cream cheese
1-1/2 cups granulated sugar

2 tablespoons white rum
1 teaspoon dark vanilla
1 teaspoon salt
4 eggs
1 egg yolk
1 pint sour cream
1/4 cup granulated sugar
1 teaspoon white rum

Crust:

1. Combine graham cracker crumbs, sugar and melted margarine until well blended. Press evenly into a 10-inch cake pan.

Batter:

1. Plump raisins in water.

2. Soften cream cheese and sugar and mix with a paddle until softened.

3. Add rum, vanilla and salt. Mix well.

4. Add eggs, one at a time, mixing on low speed until blended through.

5. Drain and add raisins and mix on low speed until just incorporated.

6. Bake at 350 degrees for 40-45 minutes. Remove and let cool.

Topping:

1. Combine sour cream, sugar and rum.

2. Spread over cheesecake and chill for service. Serves 12.

Almond Tart A La Cross Keys

1 pie crust

1 pound heavy whipping cream

6 ounces granulated sugar

1/8 teaspoon almond extract

1 tablespoon Grand Marnier

4 ounces sliced almonds, toasted

1 cup heavy whipping cream, whipped

1/4 cup almonds, sliced, toasted

1. Place pie shell in a 9-inch springform pan. Neatly and evenly trim the edge to 1/2-inch depth.

2. Combine cream and sugar in a saucepan and warm over low heat until translucent.

3. Add the next three ingredients and blend well.

4. Pour mixture into pie shell and bake at 425 degrees for 25-35 minutes or until top is golden brown. Remove from oven and chill completely. NOTE: While baking, check for air bubbles that may form and deflate them with the top of a fork or knife.

5. Whip the cream to soft peaks. Pipe whipped cream onto each portion with a pastry bag, then garnish with toasted almond slices on the piping. Serves 12.

Fairchild's Restaurant

Dinner for Four
Crabmeat Norfolk Saute
Scallop Bisques
Caesar Salad
Veal and Shrimp Maison
Banana Foster Flambé

Wine:

With Veal and Shrimp Maison - Joseph Drouhin Premier Cru Chablis

Fairchild's Restaurant

The panoramic view of the heat of the Monroeville area sets the stage for an intimate dining experience. Located atop the Jonnet Building, Fairchild's Restaurant has proven to be a welcomed addition to this affluent Pittsburgh suburb.

Fairchild's traditional elegance is dominant throughout its three dining rooms. The excellent detail is evident from the rich oak bar and lounge to the warm decor of the dining areas. Not to overshadow a fine selection of beef and veal entrees, the wide variety of excellent seafood choices is second to none. They include Coquille St. Jacques, Baked Filet of Sole Florentine, Red Snapper Pontchartrain, and several whole Maine Lobster dishes.

Ken Aiken has managed Fairchild's from its conception and has used his many years of restaurant experience to maintain a high standard of both food and service. He has also put together a very fine variety of wines and champagnes to compliment your dinner. With all these elements working together, you are assured of an exquisite evening at Fairchild's.

4099 William Penn Highway, Monroeville
412/372-1511

George S. Aiken, President
Kenneth G. Aiken, General Manager
Jeffery Clyde, Executive Chef

Crabmeat Norfolk Saute

16 ounces jumbo lump
  crabmeat
4 tablespoons clarified butter
2 pinches seafood seasoning

4 ounces white wine
2 tablespoons whole butter for
  roux
1 tablespoon parsley

1. Mix clarified butter, crabmeat and seasoning. Saute in pan over medium flame to simmer. Add wine and reduce.

2. Add roux to thicken and sprinkle with parsley.

Scallops Bisque

1 pound fresh sea scallops
2 bay leaves
Pinch salt
1/2 cup Sherry brandy
1 teaspoon spanish paprika
2 ounces Swiss cheese
4 ounces strong chicken stock
  or fish stock

1/2 teaspoon worcestershire
  sauce
1/2 teaspoon Louisiana hot
  sauce
1 pinch chopped parsley
2 ounces flour
2 ounces butter
1/2 quart whipping cream

1. Place butter and scallops in saucepan. Saute scallops, stirring with wire whip.

2. After scallops are blanched, add flour and paprika and cook for five minutes, making sure scallops do not stick. (Scallops will break up while stirring.)

3. Add wine and simmer for 5 minutes, stirring constantly.

4. Add remaining ingredients and stir until soup boils, simmer for five minutes.

5. Ladle soup into bowls and add a teaspoon of whole butter to top of each bowl of soup. Sprinkle with paprika and serve.

Caesar Salad

1 large wooden salad bowl
2 large heads Romaine
  lettuce, torn into bite size
  pieces
4 cloves garlic
4 anchovy filets
2 eggs
1 teaspoon horseradish
1 teaspoon dry mustard

Tabasco sauce
Worcestershire sauce
2 lemons
3 ounces salad oil
2 tablespoons wine vinegar
1 teaspoon black pepper
1 cup Parmesan cheese
1 cup croutons

1. Chop garlic and anchovy filets and place in wooden bowl. Rub inside of bowl with chopped mixture, then remove excess.

2. Place raw eggs in hot water and coddle. Add horseradish and dry mustard to bowl.

3. Add 4 shakes of Tabasco sauce and 4 shakes of worcestershire sauce. Squeeze juice from 2 veiled lemons and add salad oil and wine vinegar.

4. Grind in black pepper and add the coddled eggs. Add Parmesan cheese and mix.

5. Finally, add lettuce and toss gently. Garnish with croutons and serve.

Veal and Shrimp Maison

16 ounces veal, thinly sliced
8 large shrimp, peeled and
*   deveined*
10 large mushrooms, sliced

8 scallions, sliced
8 ounces chicken stock
6 ounces sweet Marsala wine
8 slices Monterey Jack cheese

1. Flour veal and add to clarified butter in large saute pan. Quickly brown both sides.

2. Add shrimp, mushrooms and scallions. Saute and deglaze by adding Marsala wine.

3. Reduce, then add chicken stock.

4. Reduce a little more and add roux to thicken.

5. Serve after melting Monterey Jack cheese over each serving, either in oven or broiler.

Banana Foster Flambé

2 whole bananas, sliced
1/4 pound butter
3/4 cup chopped walnuts
1/2 cup brown sugar
Banana liqueur

Myer's dark rum
2 pints French vanilla ice
  cream
2 tablespoons cinnamon

1. Preheat saute pan and add butter and sliced bananas, stirring continually. Add walnuts and brown sugar, stir and heat until sugar dissolves.

2. Move contents to rear of pan. Place front edge of pan to flame and heat for 20-30 seconds.

3. Pull pan from flame and add 2 ounces Banana liqueur. Place pan back on flame and prepare for flambe. Repeat with rum.

4. While rum is still aflame, sprinkle cinnamon in for flavor and effect. Once flame subsides, turn off burner and let set for 15 seconds.

5. Serve over French vanilla ice cream.

Georgetowne Inn

Dinner for Six
Artichoke Hearts Stuffed with Crabmeat and Bleu Cheese
Cheese and Beer Soup
Spinach Salad with Hot Bacon Dressing
Sole Oscar
Chilled Cheesecake with Strawberries

Wine:

With Sole Oscar - Robert Mondavi Chardonnay, 1981

George S. Aiken, Proprietor
Jeffery Clyde, Executive Chef

Georgetowne Inn

GEORGETOWNE INN'S scenic location atop Mount Washington is the perfect vantage point to view the skyline of the Pittsburgh's Renaissance.

George Aiken first had thoughts of grandeur in 1948 standing atop Mount Washington overlooking Pittsburgh's Golden Triangle surrounded by three famous rivers.

In 1974, his dreams came true. George wanted an affordable restaurant unlike the five French cuisine restaurants that were already established in Mount Washington. George combined American cuisine and a breathtaking view with moderate prices to make the Georgetowne Inn a truly great restaurant.

Our soup of the day is always one of the highlights of your meal. They range from such classics as Wedding Soup or Onion Soup to a variety of Chef Jeffery Clyde's Cream Soups. Entrees include such dishes as Veal Piccata, Veal Romano, Broiled Sole with Crabmeat, the Inn's Fisherman's Platter, or a thick tender cut of either filet mignon or New York strip steak.

The rustic warm atmosphere is the perfect environment to enjoy the generous portions of the many entrees. The friendly staff are anxious and efficient in their efforts to serve Georgetowne Inn customers.

1230 Grandview Avenue, Mount Washington
412/481-4424

Artichoke Hearts Stuffed with Crabmeat and Bleu Cheese

1 16-ounce can pasteurized crabmeat
1 tablespoon Louisiana hot sauce
1 tablespoon worcestershire sauce
Juice from 1 lemon
3 tablespoon heavy mayonnaise
2 whole eggs

1 teaspoon dry mustard
3 tablespoons white wine
3 tablespoons heavy cream
9 slices white bread
3/4 to 1 cup Bleu cheese crumbles
2 pinches black pepper
3 8-1/2 ounce cans artichoke hearts

1. Mix hot sauce, worcestershire, lemon juice, mayonnaise, eggs, dry mustard, white wine, and black pepper together in mixing bowl.

2. Cut crust of bread off and cut bread into little squares. Add to mix above.

3. Let stand while checking crabmeat for shells. Add Bleu cheese crumbles and heavy cream and mix together, then add to mix above.

4. Now add crabmeat. Stuff crabmeat mix into artichoke hearts. Top with lemon, butter, and white wine.

5. Bake at 450 degrees for 15 - 20 minutes or until crabmeat browns.

Georgetowne Inn

Cheese and Beer Soup with Croutons

1-1/2 pint heavy whipping
cream
5 ounces sharp Cheddar
cheese
17 ounces American cheese
6 ounces imported beer
4 ounces chicken stock

1/2 tablespoon chopped fresh
parsley
2 tablespoons whole butter
1/4 tablespoon Louisiana hot
sauce
1/4 tablespoon worcestershire
sauce
1/2 loaf day old French bread

Croutons:

1. Cut day old French bread into small chunks. Combine butter with
   a pinch of each: garlic salt, black pepper and basil in medium skillet.
   Heat on low flame.

2. After butter melts, add croutons. Saute for 3 minutes. Place on
   baking sheet and bake in oven at 400 degrees until brown, turning
   occasionally.

Soup:

1. Put heavy cream on low heat, stirring with wire whip. Cut cheese
   into slices or grate, then begin adding to cream, stirring constantly,
   letting cheese melt before adding more.

2. Once cheese is melted, add chicken broth, hot sauce, beer, and
   chopped parsley for color.

3. Simmer for 2 minutes, then add slices of whole butter (to keep film
   from forming).

4. Serve soup topped with croutons.

Spinach Salad with Hot Bacon Dressing

32 ounces spinach
12 strips bacon, diced
1 medium onion

8 ounces cider vinegar
1/2 cup salad oil
1 cup granulated sugar

1. Brown diced bacon in skillet, then add diced onion and simmer for two minutes.

2. Next, add cider vinegar, oil, and sugar and bring to a boil and reduce until syrupy. Add any additional vinegar or sugar to taste.

3. Wash and destem spinach and serve while dressing is still warm.

Georgetowne Inn

Sole Oscar

2 pounds fresh sole
24 ounces jumbo crabmeat
18 large pieces fresh
  asparagus
6 egg yolks
Lemon juice from 3 lemons
20 ounces butter

Pinch white pepper
Pinch salt
1/2 teaspoon worcestershire
2 teaspoons Louisiana hot
  sauce
White wine for poaching

Hollandaise Sauce:

1. Eggs must be at room temperature. Drawn butter must be hot, 180 degrees.

2. Separate eggs. Put yolks in warmed bowl. Using wire whip, start adding butter very slowly, whipping continually (do not stop whipping when adding butter). Caution: Sauce will break down if butter is added too fast. Also, you can thicken sauce by adding more butter and the converse is also true.

3. When desired texture is obtained, add lemon juice, pepper, hot sauce, worcestershire, and salt.

Sole Oscar:

1. Blanch asparagus, keeping it crisp.

2. Poach sole in white wine. When sole is almost done, add jumbo crabmeat and asparagus to warm.

3. Place sole on plate. Then put jumbo crabmeat and asparagus on top of sole in that order.

4. Top with Hollandaise sauce and serve.

Chilled Cheesecake with Strawberries

3 tablespoons melted butter
3/4 cup graham cracker
  crumbs
Sugar
1/4 teaspoon cinnamon
1/4 teaspoon nutmeg
2 envelopes unflavored gelatin
2 eggs, separated

1 cup milk
1 teaspoon grated lemon rind
1 teaspoon lemon juice
1 teaspoon vanilla extract
3 cups creamed cottage cheese
1 cup whipping cream
1 pint fresh strawberries

1. Combine the butter, graham cracker crumbs, 2 tablespoons of sugar, cinnamon and nutmeg in a bowl. Press 1/2 cup of crumb mixture into an 8 or 9-inch springform pan.

2. Combine the gelatin and 3/4 cup sugar in a medium saucepan. Beat the egg yolks, then stir in the milk gradually. Stir into the gelatin mixture and place over low heat. Cook, stirring constantly, for 3 to 5 minutes or until gelatin dissolves and mixture is slightly thickened.

3. Remove from heat and stir in the lemon rind, lemon juice and vanilla extract.

4. Beat the cottage cheese with an electric mixer at high speed for 3 to 4 minutes or until smooth. Stir into the gelatin mixture, then chill, stirring occasionally, until mixture mounds slightly when dropped from a spoon.

5. Beat the egg whites until stiff, but not dry. Add 1/4 cup of the sugar gradually and beat until very stiff. Fold into the gelatin mixture, then fold in the whipped cream.

6. Turn into the prepared pan and sprinkle with remaining crumb mixture. Chill for 3 to 4 hours or until firm. Loosen side of pan with a sharp knife and release springform.

7. Serve topped with fresh strawberry slices. Serves 12.

   NOTE: An 8-cup loaf pan may be used instead of the springform pan. Grease the loaf pan lightly. Cut waxed paper to fit pan and line loaf pan. Invert onto serving plate to unmold, then remove waxed paper.

Hugo's Rotisserie

Dinner for Two

Escargot a L'Aoile

Sonny Salad

Pasta Mafalda

Lobster a L'Orange

Grand Marnier Souffle

Hugo's Rotisserie

Whether you are entertaining a romantic interlude or impressing a business associate, Hugo's serves affordable continental and American style cuisine for lunch or dinner that pleases the eye as well as the most discriminating palate...all under the watchful eye of Sonny Santarcangelo.

Lunch 11:00am to 2:00pm Monday through Friday. Dinner 5:30pm to 11:30pm seven days per week. Award winning Sunday brunch.

Hyatt Pittsburgh, 112 Washington Place
216/471-1234 or 288-9326

Escargot a L'Aoile

12 escargots, drained
1/4 teaspoon minced shallots
1/4 cup dry white wine

1/8 teaspoon minced garlic
Butter

1. Saute garlic and shallots in butter until clear and aromatic. Add escargot, toss together. Add wine and reduce to almost dry.

2. Place escargot in shells or cups. Top with herb butter and bake fifteen minutes or until bubbly at 400 degrees.

Sonny Salad

Romaine hearts
Raddichio
Bibb lettuce
3 hearts of palm, sliced
4 artichoke hearts, halved

1 roasted red pepper, julienned
1 celery heart, sliced
6 black olives, pitted
2 large mushrooms, washed
* and sliced*

1. Wash and separate leaves of Raddichio and Bibb lettuce.

2. Toss all ingredients together in light Italian dressing and artfully arrange on plate.

2. Garnish top of salad with chopped egg and/or shrimp.

Pasta Mafalda

*1/4 pound of your favorite
pasta, cooked al denté
1 cup diced tomatoes, fresh
peeled
1/2 teaspoon fresh chopped
oregano
1/2 teaspoon fresh chopped
basil*

*1/2 teaspoon minced garlic
1/4 cup heavy cream
Parmesan cheese, fresh grated
Parsley, chopped
Pepper to taste, fresh ground
Salt to taste
2 tablespoons olive oil*

1. Saute oregano, basil and garlic in olive oil until aromatic. Add tomatoes and simmer.

2. Crush tomatoes lightly with back of spoon. Add parsley, salt, pepper, and Parmesan cheese. Finish with heavy cream.

3. Cook and drain pasta, rinse lightly. Toss together with sauce. Serve on preheated plate, top with more Parmesan cheese.

Lobster a L'Orange

2 4-ounce lobster tails
2 whole eggs
Romano cheese
Touch of cream
3 ounces orange juice

1 ounce Triple Sec or
  Cointreau
1 ounce whole butter
2 ounces all-purpose flour
Parsley, chopped
2 orange or lemon slices

1. Beat together eggs, Romano cheese and cream.

2. Steam lobster tails in shell about 15 minutes. Cool and peel shell, do not cut through meat.

3. Slice tails into medallions (about 5-6 slices) from each tail. Dredge medallions in flour, then egg batter. Saute golden on both sides. Keep warm.

4. Reduce orange juice and liqueur in shallow pan.

5. Lightly flour 2-1/2 ounce pieces of butter and add to simmering liquid in small pieces until liquid thickens.

6. Arrange lobster medallions on plate. Spoon on small amount of sauce and garnish with orange and/or lemon slices and chopped parsley.

Hugo's Rotisserie

Grand Marnier Souffle
(Serves Six)

4 ounces all-purpose flour	*1 pint whole milk*
5 ounces sugar	*8 whole eggs*

1. You'll need six 4-inch casseroles, 2-inches deep with straight sides (if the sides were rounded, the souffle would eventually break). The whole idea of the souffle is to capture the expanding air from the egg whites. The egg whites are the key, you want to pull them into the batter, you don't want to destroy that. That's what rises.

2. Butter the casseroles with clarified butter, using a pastry brush. The sides and the bottom have to be coated. Sugar the casseroles with granulated sugar. There shouldn't be any bare spots. Be careful once you sugar the casseroles not to touch the tops or the rims. The souffles will rise on one side and be lopsided if there are bare spots.

3. Mix flour and sugar with 2 whole eggs, stir until smooth with a whisk. Heat milk, do not scald, using a heavy bottomed stainless steel pan.

4. Separate six remaining eggs, yolks and whites (set aside). Pour heated milk into flour mixture. Return heated milk and flour mixture to the pot, cook it *very slowly*, stirring constantly with a whip to avoid lumps. NOTE: do not scrape the sides and especially the bottom of the pot, milk has a tendency to stick on the bottom. You don't want to get that scorching into the batter.

5. Cook until it's thick, stirring constantly, until it reaches a heavy cream sauce consistency. When it becomes heavier than a custard, do away with the whip and stir it with a wooden spoon. Continue with the wooden spoon, stir until you see the batter coming away from the sides.

6. Remove it from the heat. Stir in six egg yolks, two at a time. Put ingredients in a glass or stainless steel bowl. Place in an ice bath to cool batter down fast and keep stirring until it's cool. Stirring prevents skin from forming on the top. Batter may be stored for as many as three or four days at 35 degrees. Use immediately for best results.

7. Whip 6 egg whites, 1 egg white per souffle. Fold them together with the batter very gently. When everything is folded together, of smooth consistency and it all looks the same, pour into casseroles 3/4 to 4/5 of the way full.

8. Place casseroles on small sheet pan and bake at 400 degrees (450 degrees in a regular oven) for 15 minutes.

Grand Marnier Sauce

2 scoops ice cream (French Vanilla)
Puff whipped cream

1 to 1-1/2 ounces Grand Marnier

1. Blend together. You can also put some Grand Marnier in the batter, although it might just cook away.

2. Pour into gravy boat for serving and put in freezer until it is a pouring consistency, but firm.

3. Bring souffles to the table, pass the sauce. Put a hole in the top of the souffles and spoon on sauce.

Hyeholde

Hyeholde Sherry Bisque

Shrimp Hyeholde

Roast Rack of Lamb Persillé with DiJon Mustard Sauce

Bete Noir

Hyeholde

As long as fine china, silver, candlelight and sumptuous dining stir the juices; as long as wine comes from grapes; as long as women smile; the magic of romance will color our lives. Hyeholde is a case in point. For it was built to serve good food, fine wine and make a woman smile. In this high tech, hypertense time, Hyeholde remains a refuge devoted to the civilized pursuits of good living and peace of mind.

Hyeholde's magic isn't hyperbole. It is obvious to everyone who visits. There is a subtle air of easy living which is quite bewitching.

The modest goal of owners Pat and Carol Foy, is to provide the finest dining experience in this part of the world. Hyeholde uses only in-season fresh fruits and vegetables purchased daily. The meats, the fish and the poultry arrive the same day you do. The breads are baked daily.

Each weather change, each change from day to evening and from season to season graces the dark slate floors, the great waxed beams, the stained glass windows, the old European furniture and tapestries with particular tranquility.

The wines come covered in dust and straw from the finest vineyards in the world.

A recent addition to the Hyeholde experience is the Hyeholde Cabaret. Here you can taste some of the world's oldest and finest cognacs and ports and other after dinner drinks, exceptional desserts and gourmet pizzas. Cabaret entertainers include award-winning local performers, exciting new artists and nationally-known stars. Entertainment varies from sixteen-piece orchestras to jazz trios to individual singers and musicians.

Hyeholde serves lunch Monday through Friday and dinner Monday through Saturday. Private dinners and parties can be arranged for up to 100.

190 Hyeholde Drive, Corapolis
412/264-3116

Hyeholde Sherry Bisque

1 small ham hock
3/4 cup split peas
1 small bay leaf
6 cups beef stock
1/4 cup ground salt pork
3/4 cup onion, diced
1/2 cup celery, diced

2-1/2 tablespoons flour
1 cup tomato puree
1-1/4 cups hot chicken stock
1/2 cup dry Sherry
1/4 cup (1/2 stick) butter
Fresh ground pepper and salt
  to taste

1. Place ham hock, split peas, bay leaf and 4 cups of beef stock into a 4-quart pot. Bring to a boil, reduce heat and simmer.

2. In separate pan, saute salt pork until some of the fat is rendered. Add onion and celery and cook until nearly tender, stirring occasionally.

3. Add flour to make roux and cook 5-6 minutes. Add remaining beef stock gradually and stir until slightly thickened and smooth.

4. Return this mixture to pot with ham and peas and simmer until peas are soft, 1 to 1-1/2 hours. Remove ham hock and puree remaining mixture in food mill.

5. Add tomato puree and hot chicken stock. Cook over low flame. Add sherry and butter, stirring until butter is melted.

6. Season with fresh ground black pepper and strain. Add salt to taste. Serves 12.

Shrimp Hyeholde
(Serves One)

*5 shrimp, peeled and deveined
(10-15 size)
1 tablespoon Bleu cheese
1-1/2 tablespoons lime juice
1/4 cup flour, seasoned with
salt and pepper
1/4 cup heavy cream*

*1/2 teaspoon finely chopped
garlic
1/2 teaspoon finely chopped
shallots
Lime segments and finely
chopped parsley for garnish*

1. Preheat a saute pan and coat with olive oil. Dredge shrimp in flour and pat off excess. Place shrimp in saute pan, brown and turn.

2. Add garlic, shallots and bleu cheese. Deglaze pan with lime juice and simmer until cheese is incorporated.

3. Add cream, bring to boil and season with salt and pepper.

4. Garnish with lime segments and parsley.

Roast Rack of Lamb Persillé
(Serves Two)

1 hotel rack of lamb (to 8-pounds), split with chine bone removed (your butcher will do this for you)

1 ounce whole rosemary leaves
Salt and pepper to taste

Batter:
4 egg yolks

4 ounces dry white wine
3 ounces DiJon mustard

Breading:
2 ounces fresh chopped parsley
1 ounce fresh chopped garlic

12 ounces fresh, grated white bread (no crusts)
Salt and pepper to taste

1. The batter and breading for this dish may be prepared in advance and refrigerated. For the batter, combine egg yolks, white wine and mustard in mixing bowl, blend well, cover and refrigerate. For breading, chop parsley and garlic very fine and add to grated bread. Season with salt and pepper to taste, cover and refrigerate.

2. Remove all external fat and deckle from lamb, including the blade found on one side. The eye of the rack with bones attached will remain. Using a sharp knife, cut down and back up between each bone to remove meat between bones. You should have four bones per serving. Cut extra bones from end and reserve those chops for another use. Lay the meat on a baking sheet, sprinkle with rosemary and salt and pepper. Roast at 400 degrees for approximately 25 minutes. Meat should be rare. Remove from oven and cool.

3. Dip only the meat into the batter, then into the breadcrumbs. Lay each half on a foil lined baking sheet (to prevent bottom from burning). Wrap another covering of foil around the bones to prevent excessive browning. Bake at 400 degrees to desired degree of doneness. (Rare - 20 minutes; medium - 35 minutes; well - 45 minutes)

DiJon Mustard Sauce

2 ounces flour
2 ounces butter
1 quart lamb stock

2 ounces dry white wine
3 ounces Dijon mustard
White pepper and salt to taste

Stock:
2 pounds lamb bones and
  trimmings
1 onion
2 stalks celery
2 carrots

4 sprigs parsley
1 tomato
4 cloves garlic
2 bay leaves
12 whole peppercorns
2 quarts water

1. Place lamb bones in pan and roast at 450 degrees until golden brown. Remove from oven and place bones in a suitable stock pot. Pour a small amount of water into the roasting pan and bring to a boil over medium heat. Scrape pan to remove brown particles.

2. Pour into stock pot, cover with 2 quarts water. Chop the vegetables and add to the pot. Add remaining ingredients, bring stock to a boil, reduce heat and simmer 1-1/2 hours. Strain stock and discard bones and vegetables.

3. Melt butter in saucepan, stir in flour and cook until lightly browned. Whip in hot lamb stock, bring to boil, reduce and simmer for 30 minutes.

4. Add mustard and white wine, simmer 5 minutes. Strain and adjust seasonings.

5. Cover with plastic wrap and keep warm in double boiler until ready for use.

Bete Noir

3/4 cups sugar plus 1/4 cup
  sugar
1/3 cup water
6 ounces unsweetened
  chocolate

6 ounces semi-sweet chocolate
1/4 pound butter
6 eggs

1. Butter and paper a 9 inch baking pan.
2. Melt both chocolates and butter over simmering water.
3. When almost melted, in a separate pan mix 3/4 cups sugar and water and heat to boiling. Cook sugar and water mixture until thick and syrupy.
4. Pour sugar mixture into melted chocolate.
5. Beat eggs with remaining 1/4 cup sugar.
6. Slowly fold egg and sugar mixture into chocolate mixture. Mixture should thicken as eggs are added. Pour mixture into prepared pan.
7. Place pan into a larger pan (hotel pan) and pour water half way up the sides of the larger pan. Bake at 350 degrees for 1-1/2 to 2 hours.
8. Cake will be slightly undercooked when removed from oven. Allow to cool for one hour. Unmold carefully.

Glaze:
6 ounces semi-sweet chocolate   3/4 cup cream

1. Chop chocolate finely.
2. Heat cream and pour over chocolate, stir to melt.
3. Cool slightly to thicken and pour over top of cake.

White Chocolate Glaze:
1/2 pound white chocolate,   1 cup cream
  chopped

1. Scald cream and pour over chocolate. Let stand two minutes, then whisk together.
2. Serve each piece of Bete Noir on a bed of the white chocolate sauce.

Klein's

Lobster Bisque
Baked Spinach with Ricotta & Parmesan
Crabmeat Imperial
Key Lime Pie

Suggested Wines:

Silverado Chardonnay, 1987
Puligny Montrachet, Chavy 1983

Klein's

Klein's history is as rich as Klein's homemade apple strudel. It all began at the turn of the century. Pittsburgh was a gritty, hardworking town. Riverboats steamed their way up the Ohio to their docks along the Monongahela. Horses pulled fine handmade carriages down cobblestone streets. Immigrants arrived daily to man the mills and mines. Newfangled electric streetlights lit the way through a city darkened by soot. It was then, in 1900, that Hannah and Joseph Klein opened the doors of their restaurant for the first time. They came from the old country to make their fortunes. Hannah brought to Pittsburgh her treasured Hungarian recipes, many of which we still make and serve today. Joseph brought his European charm and personality that could brighten your spirits even on the blackest, sootiest Pittsburgh day. Together, they were quite a success, and Klein's soon became a rendezvous for Pittsburghers, travelers and celebrities. Al Jolson and Eddie Cantor frequently came to Pittsburgh to perform. They were at Klein's so often that they became close friends of Joe and Hannah.

As Klein's restaurant grew, so did Klein's family. Hannah and Joseph's children, Sidney, Virginia and Sam were now helping run things. Then, in 1932, the family made the most significant decision since opening the restaurant. They decided to specialize in fresh seafood, a unique first for Pittsburgh. They hired a skilled New Orleans chef and suddenly, Klein's meant seafood. By the end of World War II, Klein's restaurant was bigger and more popular than ever before. It was then that Sidney's son, John, turned in his Navy blues for his kitchen whites, and the third generation was on his way to learning the tradition of Klein's excellence.

When you come to Klein's today, you'll see pictures of Hannah and Joseph on the wall in the main dining room, but you'll be greeted by Ned and JoAnn. They are the fourth generation of the family. And though much about Pittsburgh and Klein's has changed since 1900, Ned and JoAnn are here to make sure two things never change: you'll always get food that's hot and good...and a smile that's warm and friendly. Our fifth generation is now in training to carry on into the 21st century!

330 Fourth Avenue
412/232-3365

Lobster Bisque

2 1-pound lobsters
1 quart of Half-and Half
  cream
1 cup rendered lobster broth

5 tablespoons flour
5 tablespoons butter, melted
2 tablespoons sherry
Few drops of yellow coloring

1. Boil lobsters in 2 quarts of boiling water with celery, onion and bay leaf for approximately 7 minutes.

2. After the water boils, reserve 1 cup of broth.

3. Remove meat from lobster and cut into chunks.

4. In a large soup pot, melt butter and add flour. Cook, but do not brown, approximately 3 minutes. Slowly add cream and stir constantly until it almost comes to a boil.

5. Add lobster broth, base, sherry and food coloring.

6. Add salt, more sherry for individual taste.

7. Add lobster meat, bring to a boil.

8. Serve hot with parsley garnish.

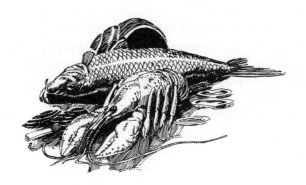

Klein's

Baked Spinach with Ricotta & Parmesan

10 ounce package of frozen
  spinach, chopped and
  drained
3 tablespoons butter, melted
2 eggs
3/4 cup Ricotta cheese
1/2 cup plus 2 tablespoons
  Parmesan cheese

1/2 teaspoon garlic, chopped
1/2 teaspoon salt
1/4 teaspoon pepper
1/4 cup plus 2 tablespoons
  seasoned breadcrumbs
3 cup souffle dish, buttered

1. Preheat oven to 350 degrees.

2. Combine all ingredients until well blended, reserving the two tablespoons of breadcrumbs and Parmesan.

3. Place in souffle dish. Combine reserved cheese and crumbs, sprinkle over top. For a crustier top, add more.

4. Bake at 350 degrees for 40-45 minutes until golden brown.

Crabmeat Imperial

1 pound of Backfin crabmeat
3 tablespoons butter, melted

1/2 teaspoon celery salt
5 tablespoons mayonnaise

1. Preheat oven to 350 degrees.

2. Mix butter, celery salt and mayonnaise in small bowl.

3. Add crabmeat, gently mix so lump crabmeat is not broken in small pieces.

4. Divide and shape in 4 balls and place in ramekins or crab shells. Bake 25-30 minutes or until golden brown.

5. Serve with lemon wedges.

Key Lime Pie

Pie Crust:
1 9-inch graham cracker pie
  shell
    OR
2 cups of fine graham cracker
  crumbs

8 tablespoons butter, melted
3 tablespoons brown sugar
Cinnamon to taste

1. Mix all of the above ingredients together and press into a 9-inch pie pan.

2. Bake at 350 degrees for 5-8 minutes, then cool.

Filling:
3 egg yolks

1 14-ounce can Eagle Brand
  Condensed milk
1/2 cup fresh lime juice

1. Beat egg yolks with mixer until very thick and pale yellow. Add condensed milk to yolks and fold into mixture.

2. Add lime juice to mixture and fold in. Pour filling into pie shell and refrigerate for at least 4 hours.

3. Top with whipped cream and lime zest.

Le Pommier

Dinner for Four

Salmon Chowder with Morels

Grilled Sweetbread with Cepe Butter

Provencal Grilled Tomatoes

Le Pommier

In 1984, the year it opened, Le Pommier won Pittsburgh Magazine's Best New restaurant Award. In 1988, under the direction of Chef Richard Larson, Le Pommier captured the Pittsburgh's Best French Restaurant Award. Chef Larson's extensive regional specialties also garnered Le Pommier a special award in 1988, Best Regional French Restaurant.

Owner Christine Dauber has remained true to her vision of a gracious, country French restaurant. Le Pommier's warm walnut wainscoting, antique lace curtains and intimate tables lit with small brass oil lamps are reminiscent of a converted French farmhouse.

Whether a traditional French meal of pate de fois gras, consomme de champignons sauvages and ris de veau aux cepes or a simple salade verte and cassoulet are more to your taste, Le Pommier's varied menu will delight you. Although Chef Larson's many seasonal specials change daily, a selection of fresh fish, veal and duck entrees and homemade soups, bread and desserts are always available.

Dr. James Dauber offers an extensive wine cellar featuring over 120 French wines and Armagnacs. A large selection of splits enables even a party of two to order an appropriate wine with each course.

Chef Larson states that "Le Pommier appeals to people who have travelled and who know good food."

2104 East Larson Street
412/431-1901

Salmon Chowder with Morels

1 pound skinless, boneless
salmon filet
3 shallots, minced
1 bay leaf
10 small red potatoes
1 cup fish stock

1 cup whole milk
1/2 cup cream
1 tablespoon butter
Pinch of fresh tarragon
Salt and pepper
Morels

1. If using dried morels, rehydrate them in water. When fully softened, saute them in butter and set aside.

2. Steam the potatoes gently in a single layer. Reserve until later.

3. In a saucepan, saute the shallots until they are clear, a few minutes. Be careful not to brown them.

4. Add the fish stock, bay leaf, milk, cream, potatoes and morels. Bring to a boil, then reduce the heat to a simmer.

5. Now add the salmon that has been cut up into 1 to 1-1/2 inch pieces and cook approximately 3 to 5 minutes. Do not overcook.

6. Garnish with tarragon.

Grilled Sweetbread with Cepe Butter

4 whole sweetbreads
Olive oil
1 ounce dried cepes
1/2 pound butter
1 cup chicken stock

1 teaspoon worcestershire
 sauce
Salt and pepper
1 clove garlic
Fresh thyme, chopped

1. Blanche the sweetbreads in boiling water for 5 minutes. Drain and cool them under cold water. Peel off any membrane or fat from them. Put in refrigerator until ready.

2. In a skillet, boil the chicken stock with the cepes. When the mushrooms have softened, remove them, but continue to boil the stock until volume has reduced to 2 tablespoons.

3. Put mushrooms, butter, and reduced stock into the food processor and process until smooth. Season with worcestershire sauce and salt and pepper.

4. Light a fire in your grill or heat your broiler.

5. Rub the sweetbreads with the garlic clove and brush with the olive oil. Grill or broil until they are golden brown, about 20 minutes.

6. Just before removing from the grill, spread the mushroom butter on the sweetbreads and allow to soften. Sprinkle with the thyme.

Provencal Grilled Tomatoes

4 medium tomatoes
3 cloves of garlic, minced
3 tablespoons chopped parsley

2 tablespoons breadcrumbs
Salt and pepper
3 tablespoons olive oil

1. Light a fire in your grill or turn on the broiler.

2. Cut each tomato in half horizontally and gently remove the seeds by squeezing from the sides. Turn cut side down on a paper towel and allow to drain.

3. In small mixing bowl, combine the garlic, breadcrumbs, parsley and a pinch of salt and pepper. Pour 2 tablespoons of olive oil into crumb mixture.

4. Brush the tomatoes inside and out with the remaining olive oil. Spoon the crumbs into the tomato halves and place on the grill.

5. Cover and allow to cook until heated through, approximately five minutes.

Lemont Restaurant

Shrimp Minuette

Bibb Lettuce with Raddichio

Grilled Chicken Breast Dijonaise

Souffle du Jour

Lemont Restaurant

The LeMont Restaurant sits atop Mount Washington. It is spanned with 10-foot windows covering the entire restaurant which gives our guests a spectacular panoramic view! We have been in the business for twenty-eight years and plan to be here for another twenty-eight years.

Our menu selections range from Regional Italian to Classic French. We have a very broad wine selection as well - 104 choices! The LeMont is one of Pittsburgh's premier restaurants. To make our guests feel special, we have mastered the art of fine food preparation along with professional, courteous service.

Come join us in CELEBRATION OF OUR 28TH YEAR
of pleasing people!

LeMont - "where light-up night is every night!"
LeMont - "romance is still alive!"

Open 4:00pm daily. Extensive bar area. Available for luncheon and dinner banquet of up to 500. Valet parking. All major credit cards accepted.

1114 Grandview Avenue, Mount Washington
412/431-3100

Shrimp Minuette (Cold Appetizer)

5 shrimp, 21-25 per pound size
3 ounces leaf lettuce, chopped
2 ounces red pepper, julienne

2 ounces green pepper, julienne
2 ounces carrots, julienne

Marinade and Dressing:
2 ounces Poupon mustard
6 ounces olive oil
2 egg yolks
1 ounce basil
Salt to taste

Black pepper to taste
Tabasco to taste
1 ounce LeMarne vinegar
1 ounce lemon juice
1/2 ounce worcestershire
sauce

1. Emulsify eggs and oil, add lemon juice and vinegar, add mustard, and remaining ingredients.

2. Toss shrimp and vegetables separately and let marinate 20 minutes.

3. Place lettuce on plate and put vegetables, then shrimp on top, place thinly sliced tomatoes around rim of plate.

Bibb Lettuce with Raddichio

Bibb lettuce

2 ounces gorgonzola vinegar
(per serving)

Dressing:
3 ounces pure olive oil
5 ounces vegetable oil
3 ounces Regina red wine
vinegar
1 ounce fresh lemon juice
1 tablespoon capers, chopped

1 teaspoon worcestershire
sauce
1 teaspoon garlic, minced
Salt to taste
Ground black pepper to taste
1/2 teaspoon dry mustard

1. Mix well.

2. Add 3/4 cup shredded imported Bleu cheese, crumble and put in dressing. Yields 12 ounces of dressing.

Grilled Chicken Breast Dijonaise
(for one)

1 6-8 ounce breast of chicken
1/2 cup oil
1/4 cup fresh lemon juice

1/2 teaspoon fresh ground
* black pepper*

Sauce:
3 teaspoons tarragon vinegar
2 teaspoons dry white wine
1 teaspoon tarragon

1/2 teaspoon ground white
* pepper*
2 teaspoons Dijon mustard
1/2 pound butter

1. Marinate chicken in oil, lemon juice, and pepper.

2. Grill chicken until done.

3. Combine vinegar and white wine in small pan, reduce to two teaspoons.

4. Remove, add tarragon and pepper, whisk in butter until thick, whisk in mustard.

5. Pour over grilled chicken, serve immediately.

Souffle du Jour

4 cups milk
1-1/2 cups sugar
1-1/2 cups flour
10 pieces of pattie butter

8 ounces liqueur (32 cents
* ounce)*
11 yolks and whites

Sauce:
Lemon zest
Orange zest

3 scoops vanilla ice cream
20 ounces whip cream

1. Prepare a dessert souffle.

2. Serve with sauce.

1902 Landmark Tavern

Dinner for Two
Tony Salad
Oysters Florentine
Seafood MacArthur

1902 Landmark Tavern

This tavern was originally established in 1902 as the Dimling Brothers Bar and Grill.

The liquor license issued by the State holds the certificate number R-8. Meaning? The 8th license issued by the State of Pennsylvania.

Painstaking care has been taken to bring back the original tiles, replace the brass and woodwork dating back to the turn of the century.

Working from old photographs, craftsmen have restored the tile patterns, brass work and tin ceilings as closely as possible. The original bar no longer existed, so a search began for a similar style. Eventually, an authentic 19th century bar was located in an old hotel in South Fork, Pennsylvania. It was purchased, dismantled and shipped to Pittsburgh where it has been refinished to add to the authentic flavor of the Tavern.

Located in Pittsburgh's bustling Market Square, the exterior was restored to its original architecture, thus completing the Tavern's addition to Renaissance II.

24 Market Square
412/471-1902

Tony Salad

Bed of leaf lettuce
3 tomato slices, arranged
  across the lettuce
3 artichoke halves

3 imported hearts of palm
  sticks, chopped
5 medium pitted black olives
Vinaigrette dressing (your
  choice)

1. Arrange the ingredients on the bed of lettuce.

2. Serve with dressing on the side.

Oysters Florentine

8 Blue Point oysters
1 small onion
10 ounces fresh spinach
3 bacon strips
1/8 teaspoon white pepper

3 minced garlic cloves
3 tablespoons unsalted butter
1 tablespoon dry sherry
Romano cheese, grated
Lemon wedge

1. Shuck the oysters, leave them in the deep shell. Place oysters in a casserole dish and refrigerate.

2. Finely chop bacon, onion and spinach (remove stems). Saute bacon until fat is rendered, add butter, onion, pepper, garlic, and sherry.

3. Saute until onions are translucent. Remove from fire and add spinach and fold.

4. Take mixture and completely cover each oyster.

5. Bake at 450 degrees for five minutes, remove.

6. Sprinkle lightly with Romano cheese, bake until cheese is browned.

7. Serve with lemon wedges.

Seafood MacArthur

1 small onion
1 small green pepper
1 large or 3 small mushrooms
8 ounces "1902" marinara
sauce
Crushed red pepper (added to
taste)

4 ounces small shrimp, peeled
and deveined
4 ounces bay scallops or sea
scallops, chopped in quarters
10 ounces imported linguini,
cooked

1. Chop onion, green pepper and mushrooms into small strips.

2. Saute vegetables in marinara sauce, add pepper after 2-3 minutes.

3. Add shrimp, saute two minutes.

4. Add scallops, saute 1-1/2 minutes.

5. Add linguini, continue to cook.

6. Serve immediately.

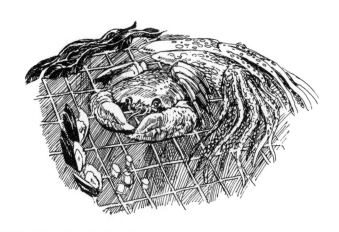

Piccolo Mondo

Dinner for Four

Sea Scallops with Pignolia Nuts and Leeks

Radicchio Lettuce with Orange Dressing

Veal Medallions Hunter Style

Raspberry Sabayon

Piccolo Mondo

Piccolo Mondo, meaning "Small World" is an accumulation of two people from different countries each with different experiences in other countries and the utilization of the best of these experiences and knowledge and blending them to make one of the finest restaurants in Pittsburgh.

Mr. Settembre, an owner and manager, is originally from Orte, Italy, a small town between Rome and Florence, Italy. After completing his secondary education, he went to excellent catering schools in Italy and Switzerland where he studied and trained for several years. After receiving his diploma, he moved on to put into practice, his years of learning in such countries as Germany, France, Switzerland, England and the Bahamas. Mr. Settembre, at one time was the youngest manager at the Regent Palace in London and opened the first disco in London, the Crazy Elephant, finally landing in Nassau, Bahamas for a period of 12 years after which he came to Pittsburgh, Pennsylvania in 1976. He established his reputation in the restaurant field in Pittsburgh with DeForo and sold that to open Piccolo Mondo in Foster Plaza in Greentree, Pennsylvania. It was while running DeForo that Mr. Settembre met Mr. Kremer, his future partner and chef for Piccolo Mondo.

Mr. Rudolf Kremer, originally from Holland, was sent by the Pittsburgh Culinary School as an apprentice with DeForo at the age of 17. While working there, his talents were recognized by Mr. Settembre who then proceeded to groom Mr. Kremer to become head chef. He studied intensely under Chef Albert Ughetto, traveled to Paris, France to work and study in a restaurant there, studied and worked in a restaurant in Washington, D.C., and finally went to California to round out his training. He was promoted to head chef at the excellent restaurant "La Sorgente" which Mr. Settembre opened in Seven Springs Resort. He was then called back to be head chef at DeForo, since Chef Albert had decided to take another position.

Piccolo Mondo

When Mr. Settembre was approached about opening a restaurant in Foster Plaza, Greentree, he asked Chef Kremer if he was interested in becoming not only the head chef, but a partner in the new venture as well. Thus began a marriage of talents out of which sprung a new five star restaurant.

Piccolo's main line of food is Northern Italian with a smattering of French cuisine and offers an extensive wine list with both imported and domestic wines which has been highly acclaimed. At Piccolo Mondo, a person can dine on good food with good service in a casually elegant atmosphere.

661 Anderson Drive, Greentree
412/922-0920

Piccolo Mondo

Sea Scallops with Pignolia Nuts and Leeks

1-1/2 pounds sea scallops
1/2 cup toasted pignolia nuts
1 small leek, finely sliced
1/2 cup dry white wine

1/2 cup raw butter
1 small clove garlic, finely
 diced
Clarified butter for sauteing

1. In a skillet, place enough clarified butter to saute the scallops.

2. Heat the skillet to medium-high heat. Lightly flour the scallops and put into the skillet.

3. Saute, stirring occasionally (for about 3 to 4 minutes).

4. Add garlic and pignolia nuts and toss about for about 30 seconds.

5. Add wine and let it reduce by half. Add raw butter, stirring constantly to make the sauce.

6. Serve with rice.

Orange Dressing

1/2 cup orange juice
2 cups salad oil
1 tablespoon lemon juice
2 egg yolks
1 tablespoon wine vinegar

8 celery leaves
1 teaspoon dried tarragon
 leaves
1 tablespoon orange zest

1. In a one-quart non-metallic bowl, put in the lemon juice, egg yolks, vinegar, chopped celery leaves, and tarragon. Whisk together.

2. Slowly start to add the oil in a small stream, whisking the entire time, until all of the oil is incorporated.

3. Add the orange juice little by little, then add the orange zest.

4. Cover and let sit 2 hours at room temperature or overnight in the refrigerator.

5. Serve with radicchio lettuce.

Veal Medallions Hunter Style

2 tomatoes, peeled, deseeded
   and diced
1/2 cup pitted, black olives,
   sliced
3/4 cup sliced medium
   mushrooms

1/4 cup marsala
1-1/2 cups Bordelaise sauce
Salt and pepper
Chopped parsley
12-1/2 ounces medallions of
   veal

1. Saute veal, then place 3 pieces on each plate.

2. In the same saute pan, put 2 tablespoons clarified butter. Saute the tomatoes and mushrooms for about 30 seconds.

3. Add olives and cook for 15 more seconds.

4. Add marsala, then Bordelaise sauce.

5. Season to taste.

6. Pour sauce over veal. Top with chopped parsley.

Piccolo Mondo

Raspberry Sabayon

8 egg yolks
2 whole eggs
1/2 pint fresh raspberries

1/3 cup Chambord
8 tablespoons sugar

1. In a 2-quart bowl (preferably copper lined), mash the raspberries.

2. Add the rest of the ingredients and mix well.

3. Place bowl over a double boiler and whisk over water that is barely at a simmer for about 4 to 5 minutes until a ribbon is formed when the whisk is removed from the bowl (be sure not to cook over too high heat or too long, this will result in scrambled eggs).

4. Serve with fresh raspberries and a sprig of mint in a tall glass.

The Prime House

Sausage Empanadas
Salmon Ravioli with Creamy Tomato Vodka Sauce
Swordfish Florentine
Macadamia Rum Raisin Ice Cream Pie

The Prime House

The Prime House…home of the PITTSBURGH CUT, features prime rib, choice aged steaks, seafood, poultry, and pasta. Prime rib is the signature item and a choice of three cuts are available, all carved in the room. The Prime House "Prime Rib Buffet", custom made for the Prime House, is also home to a "Tossed Salad Buffet". Featured tossed salads include the ever popular Caesar, Spinach, and Traditional House, to name a few.

The Prime House decor combines a mixture of Kelly Green and brass with just the right touch of pastels to balance its relaxing environment. Waiters and waitresses are dressed in black pants and vests, complete with bow ties and long white aprons, a traditional American uniform indicating that only the finest in beef is served.

101 Marriott Drive
412/922-8400

Sausage Empanadas with Tomato Sauce

Filling:
1 pound hot sausage
1 avocado, diced
4 ounces Jack cheese,
 shredded
4 ounces diced tomatoes

1 teaspoon cumin
1 tablespoon fresh cilantro,
 chopped
1 teaspoon lemon juice
1/2 teaspoon red pepper

1. Grind sausage, cook on stove, drain all grease.

2. Add avocado, Jack cheese, tomatoes, cumin, cilantro, lemon juice and pepper.

Dough:
2-3/4 cups all-purpose flour
3 tablespoons vegetable
 shortening

3/4 teaspoon salt
3/4 cup warm water

1. Measure flour in bowl, working in shortening. Dissolve salt in water and add to mixture.

2. Knead dough several minutes until smooth.

3. Divide dough into 8 portions and roll into balls. Then roll out into 7-inch circles, brush with water and add filling. Fold over and pinch dough in a circular motion to seal.

Fresh Tomato Sauce:
1 1-pound can diced tomatoes
 in juice
1 teaspoon fresh garlic,
 chopped fine
1 bay leaf

1 tablespoon basil leaves
1/2 teaspoon oregano
1/2 teaspoon sugar
3 ounces chicken stock
2 tablespoons red wine
Salt and pepper to taste

1. Add all ingredients and simmer for one hour.

Salmon Ravioli with Creamy Tomato Vodka Sauce

Pasta Dough:
1-2/3 cup all-purpose flour
2 eggs

1 teaspoon olive oil
Pinch salt

1. Mound flour on work surface or bowl, make well in center.

2. Add eggs, oil and salt. Gradually draw flour into center and knead until dough comes together.

3. Roll out onto sheets of wax paper to make ravioli.

Filling:
8 ounces fresh Norwegian salmon
2 tablespoons scallions, chopped
1 ounce white wine

4 ounces Asagio cheese
3 egg yolks
1 ounce heavy cream
1 tablespoon chopped parsley
1/2 teaspoon thyme
2 tablespoons salt and pepper

1. Puree salmon in food processor.

2. Add all ingredients except scallions and blend.

3. Then fold in chopped scallions and refrigerate.

Creamy Tomato Vodka Sauce:
1 tablespoon butter
1 ounce scallions
2 ounces vodka

4 ounces heavy cream
1 teaspoon green peppercorns
1/2 teaspoon salt
3 ounces diced tomatoes, seeded and skinned

1. Saute scallions, add vodka, cream, peppercorns, and salt.

2. Reduce by 1/3, strain, add tomatoes.

Swordfish Florentine

4 8-ounce swordfish steaks
2 ounces green olive oil
2 teaspoons garlic, chopped
8 ounces onions, diced
1 ounce Poupon mustard

2 tablespoons fresh dill,
 chopped
1 tablespoon capers
1 ounce chopped parsley
2 cups white wine
2 ounces whole butter

1. Saute garlic and onions until transparent.

2. Add mustard, dill, capers, parsley and wine.

3. Reduce by 1/3 and add butter to cream.

4. Pour over swordfish steaks.

Macadamia Rum Raisin Ice Cream Pie

Crust:
12 ounces Oreo cookies

2 ounces whipped butter

1. Grind Oreo cookies in food processor and add whipped butter.

2. Press on to bottom of 9-inch springform pan.

Filling:
*1/2 gallon rum raisin ice
   cream, softened*
*2 quarts Rich's Non-Dairy
   Topping, whipped*

6 ounces raisins
1 ounce rum extract
*1 pound macadamia nuts,
   coarsely chopped*
6 ounces chocolate morsels

1. Mix ice cream on low speed, add Rich's Topping, raisins, rum extract and nuts, mix for 1 minute.

2. Fold mixture into springform pan and level.

3. Melt 6 ounces of chocolate morsels and lace chocolate over top of pie in a crisscross motion.

Smitty's Restaurant and Lounge

Seafood Chowder

Stuffed Roast Duck Legs with Cabbage

Potato and Corn Skillet Cake

Warm Lobster Salad with Fresh Herb Beurre Blanc

Apple Tart

Wine:

Bouchaine Chardonnay 1985

Ravenswood Zinfandel 1984

Smitty's Restaurant and Lounge

Smitty's Restaurant and Lounge, located on the banks of the Monongahela River, in Speers, Pennsylvania, opened for the first time in the early summer of 1984. The owners, Dr. Alan Renton and Dr. Kutub Saifee, long-term friends, benefited from the assistance of their friend, Master Chef Byron Bardy. With Mr. Bardy's guidance, they obtained the services of culinary school-trained Chef William Hunt, whose culinary mentors included Ferdinand Metz, Paul Prudhomme, and Master Chef Byron Bardy, who acted as chief consultant prior to the restaurant's opening. Mr. Hunt orchestrated and developed a menu focused on American regional taste — he regularly changes the menu to take advantage of the marketplace.

Smitty's was completely destroyed by flooding of the Monongahela River in November 1985. Through the outstanding efforts of its owners and personnel, it has been rebuilt to be even larger. During the summer, in addition to the large glass-enclosed dining room, dinners are offered outdoors with seating on a large awning-covered deck right on the water, allowing an impressive view of a large marina, also owned by Drs. Renton and Saifee. Smitty's has been favorably reviewed in its short history by a variety of publications, including Pittsburgh Magazine, has been visited recently by the Phantom Diner and has been featured on the Evening Magazine TV program in the Pittsburgh area. Smitty's has been rated this year by the Mobil Travel Guide.

110 River Road, Belle Vernon
412/483-6900

Seafood Chowder

1/2 pound bacon, sliced
1 large onion, diced
1/4 cup butter, unsalted
3 cloves garlic, minced
1 teaspoon thyme
1/2 cup flour
3 potatoes, diced, cooked
1 pound Bay scallops

1 No. 5 can chopped clams in
 juice
6 ounces baby shrimp
6 ounces crabmeat
3 cups water
2 cups heavy cream
Pinch cayenne pepper
Salt to taste
Parsley to garnish

1. Place scallops, shrimp and clam juice in soup pot, cover with cold water on medium heat.

2. In separate frypan, saute bacon until crispy. Strain, reserve bacon.

3. In a third soup pot with heavy bottom, saute onion in bacon fat until tender. Add garlic, thyme, and butter. Saute 2 minutes.

4. Add flour for roux. Whisk in strained, hot fish stock. Bring to simmer for 5 minutes.

5. Add cream, bring back to simmer.

6. Add seafood, clams, and bacon. Bring back to simmer.

7. Serve in large rimmed soup bowls with chopped fresh parsley.

Potato and Corn Skillet Cake

*6 potatoes, 100 ct., bake, split,
  sieved
1 onion, diced fine
1 green and red pepper, diced
  fine
2 teaspoons garlic, minced
2 tablespoons butter
2 cups corn, cooked
1 cup cream*

*1/2 teaspoon thyme
Salt to taste
2 cups Cheddar cheese, grated
  or blend 2 or more cheeses
1/4 cup grated Romano for top
1 cup sour cream
1 tablespoon chives or green
  onion tops
2 eggs plus 1 egg yolk*

1. Line a buttered 12-inch skillet with the potato halves.

2. In a separate pan, saute onions, peppers, thyme and garlic until soft.

3. Deglaze pan with cream. Add corn. Bring to a simmer, remove.

4. Add the cream mixture to the sieved potatoes in a bowl. Add Cheddar cheese, 1/2 sour cream, peppers, and eggs. Mix salt to taste.

5. Fill mixture into potato shell. Top with grated Romano cheese.

6. Bake in preheated 350 degree oven for 35 minutes or until brown.

7. Whip 1/2 of sour cream to garnish, add chives.

Stuffed Roast Duck Legs with Cabbage

6 duck legs, boned
Salt, sprinkle
Black pepper, sprinkle fresh
* ground*
Fresh thyme
1 cooking apple (Granny
* Smith), peeled, seeded and*
* diced*

6 ounces Brie cheese, sliced
1 head Napa cabbage
1 tablespoon green onions,
* tops only*
5 ounces bacon, diced
3 tablespoons champagne
* stock vinegar*
5 tablespoons olive oil

1. Preheat oven to 400 degrees.

2. Combine diced apples with cheese and season with salt, pepper and thyme. Put some stuffing under skin of each duck leg.

3. Season both sides of leg with salt, pepper, and thyme. Roast for 40-50 minutes.

4. While legs are cooking, cook the bacon in a saute pan until slightly crispy. Drain off half of the bacon fat, add green onion and cabbage and saute until wilted.

5. Remove from heat and toss with vinegar and oil. Adjust seasonings.

6. Transfer to heated serving platter and serve with duck leg.

7. Garnish with cabbage leaf and fresh thyme.

Warm Lobster Salad with Fresh Herb Beurre Blanc

3 heads Boston lettuce
1 ripe avocado
Green beans, cooked
Carrots, peeled, julienned,
* cooked*
12 cherry tomatoes, peeled
6 live lobsters, cooked,
* reserved while warm and*
* shelled*
6 small red-skinned potatoes,
* steamed*
Shallots, diced fine

1 tablespoon fresh basil,
* chopped fine*
1 tablespoon fresh tarragon,
* chopped fine*
1 tablespoon fresh thyme,
* chopped fine*
1/2 cup dry vermouth
1/2 tablespoon lemon juice
8 ounces unsalted butter,
* cubed 1/2-inch*
Pinch cayenne pepper
Salt to taste

1. Arrange half a head of lettuce in serving platter.

2. Neatly arrange avocado, green beans, carrots, tomatoes, and potatoes around half the platter.

3. Slice warm lobster tail and arrange on other half of platter along with whole claws.

4. In shallow saucepan, bring to simmer the vermouth, shallots and fresh herbs. Reduce to half original volume.

5. Add lemon juice. Swirl in butter a little at a time, taking care not to *break* the butter. Pour over salad while still warm and serve immediately.

Apple Tart

Dough:
1-1/2 cups all-purpose flour
1/2 cup butter
3/4 cup confectioner's sugar
1 egg yolk
1 tablespoon milk

1. Rub together, butter, flour and sugar until walnut size lumps appear.

2. Add egg yolk and milk; knead until just incorporated. Chill.

3. Roll out dough to 1/8-inch thick. Place in tart pan.

Filling:
Apricot Glaze
4 apples (Granny Smith),
  peeled, cored and sliced
  1/8-inch thick
1/4 cup sugar
1/4 cup brown sugar
1/2 teaspoon cornstarch
1 lemon
2 tablespoons butter, melted

1. Mix sugar, cornstarch, apple and lemon juice. Let stand 10 minutes.

2. Prebake tart shell in 400 degree oven for 10 minutes.

3. Remove and brush on Apricot Glaze, arrange on shell in spiral.

4. Brush on melted butter, place back in 350 degree oven 20-30 minutes.

5. Remove, glaze again with Apricot Glaze.

Apricot Glaze:

Use apricot preserves, thinned with lemon juice, heated on the stove, and brush this on while hot.

Cinnamon Ice Cream

3 cups whipping cream
1 cup milk
1 cup sugar

1 stick cinnamon
7 egg yolks
1 teaspoon ground cinnamon

1. Heat cream, sugar, cinnamon on very low heat for 15 minutes.

2. Whisk a little hot cream into the egg yolks and then return to pan and cook over low heat until it thickens.

3. Strain, freeze in ice cream machine.

Sterling's

Portuguese Bean Soup
Sterling's Salad
Barbecue Shrimp
Apple Strudel

Sterling's

A t some hotel dining rooms, you merely eat, but at Sterling's you dine. In the elegant, yet relaxed atmosphere of a British Polo Club. Our Chef's prepare a delectable array of seafood and veal specialties, as well as steaks, chops and prime rib. The wine list is extensive, the desserts superb.

The winner of several table top awards, Sterling's is the perfect room for a special lunch or dinner. And if you're going to the theatre or symphony, dine at Sterling's and take advantage of the complimentary van service to and from Heinz Hall or the Benedum Center. Jackets are preferred. Reservations suggested.

Gateway Center
412/391-4600

Portuguese Bean Soup

10 ounces red kidney beans,
dry, washed
4 ounces navy beans, dry,
washed
4 ounces black beans (turtle
beans), dry, washed
10 cups beef or ham stock
10 ounces ham hocks or ham
trimmings
2 ounces ham, diced 1/2",
sauteed
4 ounces Portuguese sausage,
diced (or any good smoked
sausage)
12 ounces onions, diced 1/4"
12 ounces celery, diced 1/4"

12 ounces carrots, diced 1/4"
1 cup leeks, diced 1/4"
4 ounces garlic, chopped fine
2 ounces olive oil
16 ounces tomato, diced,
canned with juice
1/4 cup tomato paste
1 cup potatoes, diced 1/2"
3 ounces roux, brown
Pepper, black, ground to taste
1 1/2 tablespoons chili powder
2 bay leaves
Coriander or fresh cilantro to
taste
Salt or beef base to taste

1. Soak all beans separately in plenty of cold water overnight.

2. Strain all beans. Cover kidney and navy beans with fresh water, add ham hocks and trimmings. Cook beans until well done. Discard trimmings, remove ham hocks, cool, debone and dice meat 1/2". Separately cook black beans until well done. Strain, rinse with water and reserve.

3. Heat oil in tilting frying pan. Saute onions, celery, carrots, leeks, garlic, cabbage, and diced ham hocks without taking color, add tomato paste and blend well.

4. Fill up with stock, add kidney and navy beans with liquid, also black beans. Bring to a boil, simmer for 15 minutes.

5. Now add potatoes, tomatoes, all seasonings and roux. Blend well and simmer 30 more minutes.

6. Remove from heat, adjust seasoning, place into clean containers. Cool quickly, cover and refrigerate.

7. If soup is too thick when reheated for daily use, thin down with clear stock.

Sterling's

Sterling's Salad

1 head Romaine
4 ounces chopped walnuts

Small wheel of Brie
4 ounces favorite dressing

1. Remove the outer leaves from the Romaine, then quarter. Wash. Place on plate.

2. Sprinkle the walnuts over the top.

3. Cut Brie into 8 pieces. Place 2 wedges on each plate.

4. Dress with your favorite dressing.

5. Serve.

Barbecue Shrimp

36 pieces shrimp
6 teaspoons Old Bay Cajun
 Spice
12 ounces fresh butter

12 ounces beer
Salt and pepper, for seasoning
3 teaspoons garlic
12 ounces tomato concasse

1. Dust shrimp with flour and spice, saute in fresh butter.

2. When light pink, add garlic and deglaze with beer.

3. Stir in tomato concasse.

4. Serve with 24 ounces of rice.

Apple Strudel

12 puff pastry dough, strips
  rolled 1/8" thick (4 1/2" X
  20")
40 apples, peeled, cored,
  quartered, sliced 1/8"
2 pounds raisins, soaked,
  drained
2 pounds pecans or walnuts,
  chopped

1 pound sugar
1 teaspoon cinnamon
4 lemons, rind grated
Egg wash as needed
Cake crumbs, bread crumbs,
  graham cracker crumbs, or
  crushed corn flakes as
  needed

1. Place 3 puff dough strips on paper lined sheetpan. Brush with egg wash and cover with center 2 1/2" wide with cake crumbs.

2. Place apple filling 2 1/2" wide and 2" high on top of crumbs.

3. To cover filling, take 3 puff dough strips and make diagonal cut-ins 1/4" apart, 3" long.

4. Place strips over filling and press sides down.

5. Brush strudel with egg wash. Bake in preheated oven at 375 to 400 degrees to a golden color.

Note: Glaze warm apricot glaze or dust with powdered sugar at serving time. Serve at room temperature with vanilla custard.

The Terrace Room

*Wilted Spinach Salad with Hot Pancetta Bacon Dressing
and Roasted Walnuts*

Pineapple-Lime Sorbet

*Broiled Filet Mignon, Locatelli Cheese, Onion and
Orzo Cake, Barbaresco Wine Sauce*

*Chocolate Pasta, Fresh Berries and
White Chocolate Creme Anglaise*

The Terrace Room

The Terrace Room, located in the Westin William Penn Hotel, was built in 1916. Originally called the Italian Terrace, it is now the home of a three-meal-a-day restaurant featuring regional cuisine with a lot of Pittsburgh favorites on the menu. The dining room is open for breakfast, lunch and dinner daily. On Saturday evenings, it features a dinner dance and on Sundays, a Champagne Brunch.

The decor of the room is that of a bygone era with extremely high ornate ceilings and rich paneling, Austrian crystal chandeliers, plush banquettes, and a large mural depicting an early Pittsburgh scene, giving it an old world ambience. Reservations recommended.

530 William Penn Place
412/553-5235

Wilted Spinach Salad with Hot Pancetta Bacon Dressing and Roasted Walnuts

*1 pound cleaned, fresh
spinach*

*10 ounces Bacon Dressing
6 ounces roasted walnuts*

Hot Bacon Dressing

*2 pounds bacon, diced
8 ounces onion, diced small
8 ounces brown sugar
1/2 tablespoon fresh ginger,
chopped fine*

*1 quart malt vinegar
2 ounces salad oil
White pepper to taste
Cornstarch (to thicken lightly)
Salt to taste*

1. Saute bacon, onions and ginger.

2. Add brown sugar to caramelize.

3. Add malt vinegar and reduce.

4. Add oil, incorporate well.

5. Add salt/pepper to taste.

6. Thicken with cornstarch.

7. Garnish salad with chopped eggs (hard boiled), mushrooms and roasted walnuts.

8. Heat dressing and toss with spinach to wilt. Add garnishes and serve.

Pineapple-Lime Sorbet

2 cups pineapple juiced (fresh
   pureed pineapple)
3 tablespoons fresh lime juice

2 cups simple syrup
1 egg white

1. Mix all ingredients well.

2. Place into sorbet machine and run until set.

3. Place into freezer to hold.

4. Scoop and serve.

Broiled Filet Mignon, Locatelli Cheese, Onion and Orzo Gratin, Barbaresco Wine Sauce

6-8 ounce filet mignon
(broiled to likeness)
1/2 onion
1/2 tablespoon garlic
1/2 tablespoon olive oil

6 ounces Orzo
12 ounces beef stock
1/3 tablespoon Kosher salt
1/2 teaspoon white pepper
4 ounces Locatelli cheese

1. Heat oil, slowly caramelize onions.

2. Add Orzo and saute for two minutes.

3. Add stock and bring to boil. Reduce to simmer and cook until Orzo is very soft.

4. Place Orzo and Locatelli cheese into a buffalo chopper and chop until smooth.

5. Spread onto sheet and chill.

6. Cut into 2 inch circles.

7. Grill and place atop filet.

Barbaresco Sauce

1/2 quart Chianti wine
1/2 quart beef stock
3 cups demi glaze

4 carrots, diced small
1 onion, diced small
3 celery stalks, diced small

1. Mix wine, beef stock and demi glaze and reduce by 3/4.

2. Caramelize vegetables until dark brown color. Add to reducing stock.

3. Place sauce onto plate with filet topped with Locatelli Orzo cake.

Chocolate Pasta, Fresh Berries and White Chocolate Creme Anglaise

6 2-ounce portions of chocolate pasta formed into a bird's nest.
Fresh raspberries, strawberries, blueberries or any other seasonal fruit or

berry, tossed lightly in powdered sugar and placed inside pasta nests
10 ounces White Chocolate Creme Anglaise

Pasta:
1 cup cake flour
1 egg, beaten

1/2 cup cocoa powder
1 egg yolk
Water

1. Mix all ingredients together slowly on floured table.
2. Let rest, refrigerate for 1/2 hour.
3. Roll pasta out to 1/8 inch thickness.
4. Cut into 1/8 inch thick strips.
5. Place into boiling, lightly salted water for about 5 seconds and place back into ice water.
6. Drain water and let dry.
7. Place onto plates in form of nests.

White Chocolate Anglaise:
2 ounces white chocolate
3 egg yolks

1-1/2 ounces sugar
1-1/4 cup milk, scalded
1/2 teaspoon vanilla

1. Melt chocolate in steamtable.
2. Beat yolks and sugar for 3 minutes and slowly add scalded milk and return to heat in double boiler and cook until thick.
3. Add melted white chocolate to milk mixture and stir together.
4. Cool in ice bath.
5. Place sauce around pasta nest.
6. Garnish with fresh mint sprig.

Top of the Triangle

Shrimp Rockefeller
Strawberry Bibb Salad
Rack of Lamb with Zinfandel Sauce
Sauteed Mushrooms with Madeira
Pumpkin Cheesecake

Top of the Triangle

The Top of the Triangle offers an atmosphere of casual elegance and a breathtaking view from 62 stories above downtown Pittsburgh. The chef has created an extensive menu of specialties, including Chateaubriand, Roast Duck with Cabernet Orange Sauce, Filet Mignon, and Norwegian Salmon. Entertainment and dancing is offered nightly. There is reduced rate parking in the building after 4:00pm and all day on Saturday.

600 Grant Street, located in the USX Tower
412/471-4100

Gulf Shrimp Rockefeller

Part I:

3 tablespoons butter
3 tablespoons flour
2-1/2 cups hot milk
1/8 teaspoon worcestershire
  sauce

1-1/4 tablespoons grated
  Parmesan cheese
3/8 teaspoon salt
1/16 teaspoon pepper

Part II:

6 tablespoons butter
2-1/4 teaspoons
  worcestershire sauce
1-1/8 teaspoons salt
1 drop Tabasco sauce
1-1/2 cups raw spinach,
  chopped 1/4 inch pieces

2 tablespoons green onions,
  chopped 1/8 inch pieces
2 tablespoons celery, chopped
  1/8 inch pieces
1/4 clove garlic, chopped fine
1/4 cup finely chopped parsley

Part III:

1 pound cooked and cleaned
  shrimp

3/4 cup buttered breadcrumbs

1. Make a Cream Sauce using the 3 tablespoons butter, flour and hot milk. When the sauce thickens and flour taste disappears, add 1/8 teaspoon worcestershire sauce, Parmesan cheese, salt and pepper. Set aside temporarily.

2. Melt 6 tablespoons butter. Add worcestershire sauce, salt, Tabasco sauce, spinach, green onion, celery, garlic and parsley. Simmer until spinach wilts and other vegetables are tender, about five minutes.

3. Put 1/4 cup spinach mixture into each individual ramekin. Place 6-7 shrimp in a layer over spinach mixture and pour 1/3 cup cream sauce over shrimp. Sprinkle 2 tablespoons buttered breadcrumbs over all.

4. Bake in 350 degree oven for 15 minutes until sauce begins to bubble and crumbs are a golden brown.

Strawberry Bibb Salad
(Serves Four)

*2-3 heads Bibb lettuce,
washed and thoroughly
drained
12-16 red onion rings, 1/8
inch thick*

*3 cups strawberries, washed,
cleaned, cut in quarters
1/2 cup Celery Seed Dressing**

1. Combine strawberries and Celery Seed Dressing, stir gently to combine thoroughly.

2. Divide Bibb lettuce into 4 salad plates.

3. Arrange 3-4 onion rings slightly overlapping on top of the Bibb.

4. Place approximately 3/4 cup marinated strawberries on top of the onions.

* Celery Seed Dressing

*2 cups powdered sugar
1 tablespoon dry mustard
1 tablespoon salt
1/2 cup plus 1 tablespoon
vinegar*

*1/2 cup salad oil
1 tablespoon paprika
2 cups salad oil
1 tablespoon celery seed*

1. Combine powdered sugar, mustard, salt and vinegar. Stir well, allow to stand at room temperature for 2-3 hours until mixture is the consistency of honey. Stir every 20-30 minutes.

2. Heat 1/2 cup salad oil until just warm. Add paprika. Stir well. Strain and cool.

3. Combine paprika-oil mixture with 2 cups of salad oil and add very slowly to mustard mixture. Mix on high speed.

4. Stir in celery seeds, chill thoroughly. Makes 3 cups.

5. Bring to room temperature before using.

Roast Rack of Lamb Dijon
(Serves 6)

6 rib racks
1-1/2 teaspoon salt
3/4 teaspoon black pepper
3/4 cup Mustard Egg Batter
(recipe below)

1-1/2 cups Seasoned
   Breadcrumbs (recipe below)
1-1/2 cups Zinfandel Sauce*

1. Season racks with salt and pepper. In lightly oiled saute pan, sear to lightly brown meat on all sides. Do not cook rack in pan, only sear meat to seal in juices.

2. Remove rack from pan and cool at room temperature.

3. Dip rack in Mustard Egg Batter and drain excess batter.

4. Place rack in Seasoned Breadcrumbs to coat the meat well, pressing crumbs into meat, including the ends.

5. Place rack on pan, bone side down and bake in 350 degree oven for approximately 20-22 minutes. Rack should be served rare to medium-rare unless otherwise specified.

6. Remove meat from bone by slicing along entire rib area between bone and meat, staying along the bone. Then slice meat into 5 or 6 thin medallions.

7. On a hot dinner plate, pour 1/4 cup Zinfandel Sauce*. On sauce, place rib bones of rack with meat side facing down, curved portion facing up. Arrange meat to lay overlapping, part way on the rack and continuing onto the plate.

NOTE: Purchase Prime Rib Rack, split, chine, and feather bones removed and bones frenched. (Split racks need to be cut in half to get 12-14 ounce portions.)

Mustard Egg Batter:

1/2 cup plus 2 tablespoons
eggs, beaten

2 tablespoons Grey Poupon
mustard

1. Combine egg batter and mustard thoroughly using a wire whip.
2. Cover and refrigerate until needed.

Seasoned Breadcrumbs:

1-1/2 cups dry breadcrumbs
3 tablespoons parsley,
chopped

2 teaspoons garlic, minced
1-1/2 teaspoons Krazy salt

1. Combine all ingredients in mixing bowl, using rubber spatula.
2. Keep covered and refrigerate until needed.

* Zinfandel Sauce

1/2 cup Zinfandel wine
1 tablespoon onion, minced
1 cup Convenience Brown
Sauce, hot

3/4 tablespoon honey
2 tablespoon butter, room
temperature

1. Place wine and onion in saucepan. Bring to boil. Continue to boil until wine has reduced by approximately 1/3.
2. Add brown sauce and honey, reduce to a simmer and cook approximately 2-3 minutes.
3. Remove from heat and whip butter, 1 ounce at a time, until well blended.
4. Cover and keep hot until needed.

Mushrooms Madeira

2 pounds mushrooms, 3/4 to
  1 inch whole, cleaned
1/4 cup butter

1/2 teaspoon salt
1/4 cup Madeira
1 teaspoon chopped parsley

1. Place mushrooms and butter in pan and saute 2 minutes.

2. Add salt and wine and continue to saute until mushrooms are cooked, approximately 5-6 minutes.

3. In four fluted ramekin or casserole dishes, place 6 ounces sauteed mushrooms. Sprinkle with 1/4 teaspoon chopped parsley.

Pumpkin Cheesecake

1-1/2 cups Gingersnap cookie
  crumbs
2 ounces (1/4 cup) butter,
  melted
1 pound 8 ounces cream cheese
1-1/2 cups granulated sugar
2-1/4 cups Libby's canned
  pumpkin

1-1/4 teaspoons cinnamon
1/4 teaspoon ginger
1/4 teaspoon nutmeg
1/16 teaspoon salt
1/4 cup heavy cream
5 eggs

1. Combine cookie crumbs and butter. Press into the bottom of a 9 inch springform pan. Bake at 350 degrees for 8 minutes.

2. Beat cream cheese on medium speed until it is soft, approximately 2 minutes.

3. Slowly add sugar to the cream cheese and cream well, approximately 3 minutes.

4. Add pumpkin, cinnamon, ginger, nutmeg, salt and cream to the cream cheese mixture and thoroughly combine.

5. Add eggs one at a time. Continue to beat on medium speed for 10 minutes. Scrape bowl often.

6. Pour mixture into the springform pan and bake at 350 degrees for 1-1/4 to 1-1/2 hours or until toothpick comes out clean.

7. Loosen edge of cake with blade of knife. Let cool on rack to room temperature.

8. Remove sides of pan and refrigerate for at least 2 hours.

9. Garnish each piece with whipped cream. Serves 12.

Vernon's

Dinner for Four

Tomato Bread

Caesar Salad

Kale and Italian Sausage Soup

Cajun Veal & Shrimp Fettucini

Chicken Marsala

Fresh Strawberries 'N Cream Pie

Vernon's

At Vernon's, the menu is so extensive, you'll find a new favorite everytime you dine there! From appetizers to desserts, the variety is mouth-watering. You might start with Crispy Potato Skins or Pita Chips with Artichoke Dip or any of the 12 delicious appetizers. And the choices only get better. Double-fisted burgers and sandwiches, salads, pastas and entrees — from low calorie delights such as Pasta Primavera to Shrimp and Scallop Brochette to Prime Rib — you'll love them all! And don't forget dessert! Open seven days, serving lunch, dinner, cocktails and Sunday buffet brunch. Happy Hour Monday-Saturday nights.

395 South Hills Village
412/531-3688

Tomato Bread

4 small French rolls, cut in
  half lengthwise
1/2 cup garlic butter, soft
16 tomato slices, 1/4 inch

2 tablespoons plus 2
  teaspoons Parmesan Cheese
  Mixture*
3 cups Mozzarella cheese,
  sliced 1/16 inch

1. Spread each half of roll with 1/2 ounce garlic butter.

2. Place 2 tomato slices on each half roll.

3. Sprinkle 1 teaspoon Parmesan Cheese Mixture over tomato.

4. Arrange 1-1/2 ounce Mozzarella cheese over tomato.

5. Place half rolls (2 halves per serving) on baking tray and place in 350 degree oven 10-12 minutes or until cheese melts and starts to brown slightly.

* Parmesan Cheese Mixture

1/2 cup Parmesan cheese,
  grated
1/2 teaspoon oregano

1/2 teaspoon thyme
1 teaspoon Krazy salt

1. Combine all ingredients until well blended.

Vernon's

Caesar Salad

6 cups Romaine lettuce, 1-1/2
  inch pieces
1 tablespoon Parmesan cheese

2 tablespoons Caesar dressing
1 anchovy filet, whole
2 tablespoons garlic croutons

1. Prepare Romaine in advance, wash and cut into 1-1/2 inch pieces. Drain and refrigerate.
2. Place cut Romaine and Parmesan cheese in pan or bowl for tossing.
3. Pour Caesar dressing over Romaine-cheese mixture; toss until greens are lightly coated and cheese is evenly distributed.
4. On a chilled salad plate, place 1 portion Caesar salad. Sprinkle 2 tablespoons garlic croutons evenly over the top. Place one anchovy filet in the center of salad.

Kales and Italian Sausage Soup

1/2 pound kale, stems
  removed, cut 1/2 x 1/2 inch
1 cup diced tomatoes
1 tablespoon chicken base
2 tablespoons tomato paste
1 teaspoon basil
1/8 teaspoon thyme
1 teaspoon garlic, minced
2 cups onions, 1/2 inch diced

1/4 cup celery, 1/2 inch diced
1/2 bay leaf
1/4 teaspoon Krazy salt
1 quart and 2-1/2 cups water
1/2 pound Italian sausage,
  cooked, drained
2 cups potatoes, 1/2 inch diced
1/2 cup Parmesan cheese, for
  service

1. In saucepan, place kale, chicken base, diced tomatoes, tomato paste, basil, thyme, garlic, onions, celery, bay leaf, Krazy salt and water. Simmer 1 hour.
2. Saute Italian sausage (casing removed) in skillet, crumbling in 1/2 inch pieces. Drain thoroughly.
3. Add sausage and potatoes and simmer approximately 30 minutes or until potatoes are tender.
4. Sprinkle 2 tablespoons Parmesan cheese over 2 cup portion.

Fettucini with Veal and Shrimp Cajun Style

3/4 pound veal cutlet, pounded to 1/4 inch, cut julienne 1-1/2 x 1/4 x 1/4 inch
1/4 cup plus 1 tablespoon plus 1 teaspoon Cajun Seasoned Flour*

1 cup clarified butter
3/4 pound raw shrimp, cleaned, tails off
2 cups heavy cream
2 quarts fettucini, cooked
1/2 cup green onions, cut 1/4 inch

1. Toss veal in Cajun Seasoned Flour until coated.

2. Saute in clarified butter one minute.

3. Add shrimp, saute 1-2 additional minutes.

4. Add cream, continue to cook until cream begins to thicken.

5. Add fettucini and green onion, saute until fettucini is heated throughout.

6. Serve with grated Parmesan cheese on side.

* Cajun Seasoned Flour

1/4 cup flour
1-1/2 teaspoon salt
1-1/4 white pepper

1 teaspoon onion powder
1 teaspoon cayenne
1/2 teaspoon paprika

1. Combine all ingredients together thoroughly.

Chicken Marsala

4 pieces boneless chicken
  breasts, skin and fat
  removed, 4 ounces each
1 tablespoon margarine
1/4 cup flour
1/8 teaspoon salt

Few grains pepper
1 cup mushrooms, sliced
1/2 teaspoon garlic, minced
1/2 cup chicken broth
1/2 cup Marsala

1. Flatten each chicken breast to 1/4 inch thickness.

2. Cut in half.

3. Heat margarine in teflon skillet.

4. Combine flour, salt and pepper.

5. Dip chicken pieces into flour mixture to coat evenly, shake off excess.

6. Saute chicken breasts for 1-2 minutes until golden brown on one side.

7. Turn chicken breasts over and saute on other side for 1 minute.

8. Add mushrooms, garlic, chicken broth and Marsala.

9. Continue to cook for 1-2 minutes until mushrooms are tender and chicken is thoroughly cooked.

10. Place chicken breasts on serving platter, pour mushrooms and pan juices over the chicken. Serve immediately.

Fresh Strawberries 'N Cream Pie

Strawberry Mixture:
4-3/4 ounce (1 box)
  Strawberry flavored Danish
  dessert

1/2 cup cold water
1 cup water
1 scant teaspoon lemon juice,
  freshly squeezed and strained

1. Add cold water to Danish dessert and mix until dissolved.

2. Heat second amount of water to boiling. Add dissolved Danish dessert gradually, *stirring constantly*. Allow mixture to come back to boiling point and then remove from heat. Add lemon juice and mix well.

3. Chill, stirring occasionally, until mixture thickens to the consistency of unbeaten egg whites.

Cheese Mixture:
7 ounces cream cheese, room
  temperature
2 tablespoons granulated
  sugar

1/8 teaspoon salt
1/2 teaspoon vanilla
1 tablespoon plus 1 teaspoon
  coffee cream

1. Beat cheese until smooth and creamy. Add sugar, salt and vanilla and mix to combine.

2. Add cream gradually and beat until mixture has a good spreading consistency.

To Assemble:
1 quart ripe whole fresh
  strawberries, washed, stems
  removed
1/4 cup granulated sugar

1 baked, cooled pastry shell
1 cup (8-1/2 ounces) Cheese
  Mixture (recipe above)
1-1/2 cups Strawberry
  Mixture (recipe above)

1. Sprinkle sugar over berries and allow to stand at room temperature for 15 minutes.

2. Spread Cheese Mixture over bottom of baked pastry shell.

3. Combine *drained*, sweetened strawberries and partially congealed Strawberry Mixture and pour evenly over Cheese Mixture.
4. Chill pie 2 hours until set. Serve with a spoonful of sweetened whipped cream on top of each piece.